MW01152191

✗ June 25, 2004.

Good Food, Healthy Planet

Jan 19 – June 6, 2024

This book was written, photographed,
and produced in the area we know today
as Canada. I acknowledge the historical
oppression of these lands and cultures,
and the original peoples. I recognize the rich
history and contributions of the Indigenous
Peoples who have stewarded this land for
thousands of years. I am committed to
ongoing learning and solidarity with them
and to the healing and decolonizing journey
we are on together.

This book was written, photographed,
and produced with high regard for reducing
waste, food and otherwise.

Good Food, Healthy Planet

Your Kitchen Companion to Simple, Practical, Sustainable Cooking

PUNEETA CHHITWAL-VARMA

TOUCHWOOD

TouchWood Editions
touchwoodeditions.com

The information in this book is true and complete to the best of the author's
knowledge. All recommendations are made without guarantee on the part of the
author or the publisher.

Edited by Meg Yamamoto
Proofread by Senica Maltese
Cover and interior design by Jazmin Welch

CATALOGUING INFORMATION AVAILABLE FROM LIBRARY AND ARCHIVES CANADA
ISBN 9781771514064 (hardcover)
ISBN 9781771514071 (electronic)

TouchWood Editions acknowledges that the land on which we live and work is within
the traditional territories of the Lkwungen (Esquimalt and Songhees), Malahat,
Pacheedaht, Scia'new, T'Sou-ke and W̱SÁNEĆ (Pauquachin, Tsartlip, Tsawout,
Tseycum) peoples.

We acknowledge the financial support of the Government of Canada through the
Canada Book Fund, and the province of British Columbia through the Book Publishing
Tax Credit.

This book was produced using FSC®-certified, acid-free papers, processed chlorine free,
and printed with soya-based inks.

Printed in China

28 27 26 25 24 1 2 3 4 5

To my mom and dad, Pamila and Inder Kumar,
who together showed me how to live with
openness and abundance.

Papa, I wish you were here to see this book
come to life.

Mumma, I am thrilled to share this book with you.

For my husband, Vivek, and my children, Mahika
and Saranya; I couldn't do this without you.

Chapter 1
The Big Why

Chapter 2
The Big How

Chapter 3
How to Stock a Good Food Kitchen

Chapter 4
Recipes with All the Benefits

Preface

This book is my rallying cry to transform how we cook and what we eat. It is a collection of strategies, science-based advice, recipes, and kitchen tips that expand on the notion of good food. For years now, good food has been described as what *tastes good* and/or is *good for us*. That tells only part of the story. Defining good food in passive and self-centric terms such as how it tastes and how it affects our bodies is simply not adequate for our times.

When I first started writing this book, COVID-19 was the stuff of Hollywood movies and Robin Cook novels. The world has certainly transformed since then, and the impact of the global pandemic continues to be felt in every aspect of our lives. Along with the virus, we are facing climate chaos events in real life. Further, we are only beginning to properly acknowledge the generations of absolute inequality and injustice upon which our social and economic systems were built.

The antidote to feeling powerless is action: an urgent collective effort that will bring society forward; collective, positive action that, like so many other wonderful things, begins around the dinner table.

During the pandemic, when many of us found ourselves at home for months on end, cooking brought joy and creativity into our otherwise repetitive and lonely routines. Cooking at home, a much-maligned and mundane task, was finally trending. This was the time most of us were unlearning old habits and adopting those that would keep us, and others, safe.

When meeting friends and family and people outside our bubbles became restricted, we truly appreciated gathering with our loved ones. With forests burning and the doomsday clock ticking closer to catastrophe (when I started writing this book in 2020, it was at 100 seconds to midnight; since then, it has paused at 90 seconds to midnight in 2023[1]), we are finally seeing it is simply not enough to look out for ourselves and our families; we must also look after the planet.

That's where this book comes in. *Good Food, Healthy Planet* reveals the secrets behind making good food that is delicious, good for us, and good for the planet. Using mainly shelf-stable ingredients that are within reach for most and following simple recipes and techniques, this book provides practical advice that is based on the latest scientific evidence on gut health and its connection with mental health, as well as the impact our food choices have on the environment. This book eases the burden of decision-making at home and shows us how we can prioritize our personal well-being and the prosperity of the planet, all at the same time.

Good Food, Healthy Planet is written for people and the planet, with the best interests of both at heart. I am deeply grateful for your attention and regard in picking up this book, and I invite you on this journey toward health, happiness, and prosperity for all.

An Introduction, a Story of Root Shock, and a Love Letter of Sorts

For as long as I can remember, I have known that food is more than just fuel. When I'm feeling homesick, a mellow bowl of *khichdi* (rice and yellow lentil stew) offers me comfort and warmth. A whiff of cinnamon and cloves will uplift my mood. A pinch of fennel seeds will soothe my children's rumbly tummies. There's more to food than just the acts of cooking and eating. It nourishes our bodies and also our senses and our minds. It offers enjoyment, contentment, and an opportunity to connect around the dinner table. Food is more than just fuel, and it is far more than simply flavour; food is the sum of both, and so much more. Along with allowing us to enjoy taste, comfort, and connection, it supports healthy bodies and strong minds. Moreover, as we dig deeper into the choices we make in the kitchen, we learn that what we eat affects not only us but also the health and prosperity of our planet.

FOOD CONNECTS US

Whenever I'm out to the corner store or at the supermarket or even just picking up my morning coffee, I know it will take me longer than most other people. It's because I stop and chat. Most times it's just friendly, lighthearted talk, but there was that time I chanced upon a nugget of learning when I talked to my neighbourhood baker about sourdough bread. I didn't know then that baking sourdough bread requires many steps over multiple days to allow sufficient time, handling, and fermentation to make just one loaf of bread.

Or there was that time I struck up a conversation with the owner of a tiny grocery store about why he buys perfectly ripe strawberries at the wholesale market every morning. It's because most stores look for strawberries that are a few days away from ripe so they last the journey from market to store to people's homes. But the owner of this store, Jim, buys berries that are ready to eat because these are often left behind and end up discarded on the compost pile. You read that right: the juiciest and most luscious of the crop are often thrown away because they don't last the time that's needed for them to be stored, sold, and eaten. And so Jim buys them, even though he is aware that these perfectly ripe berries won't last the time on the shelf. Jim is a small-business owner, though, and he worries about his overhead costs, so right there, in his tiny storeroom, in the back of his shop, down the street from where I live, Jim freezes the ripest, most luscious fruits bought at their peak (instead of unripe and crisp, as many supermarkets buy their fruit). Once the fruits are frozen, he sells them by the bag to people like me. An innovative way to offer flavour, make the best of what's in season, and reduce waste, all that takes place in the backroom of a small grocery store in midtown Toronto. A story I wouldn't have learned if Jim and I hadn't started talking all those years ago.

Food connects us. I've known that for longer than I can remember. My dad was in the Indian military, so my family lived a nomadic lifestyle. The life of an army brat, as we are called, often means a new city and new school every 18 months, and my brother and I learned to adjust to this life on the go. As hard as the constant feeling of "new" was, my mom and dad made it easier by holding us together with routines that seemed odd at the time, for example eating lunch together at 3:00 PM as it was the only time after school, my mom's work, and my dad's barrack rounds that we could all be together around the table.

Living a nomadic life as a child was hard, but it was also one of the things I loved most about my childhood, mainly because India is such a higgledy-piggledy mosaic of culture, language, and cuisine, and every new city we lived in offered a fresh opportunity to try new foods and experience family traditions in a new way. Even something as subtle as the smell of the markets felt different across regions. As a young girl, I found incredible joy in the simple act of walking through strange *galliyaan* (alleys) and visiting and shopping at new markets with my mom.

Food and the stories behind it, of how it was grown and cooked and what went into making the dish, was already becoming very important to me.

THE LIFE OF A NOMAD BUT ALWAYS ROOTED IN THE KITCHEN

This nomadic style of living continued when I left home to live on my own. My hubby and I fell in love, got married, and embarked on an adventure together, uprooting ourselves from India to move to Dubai. The year was 1999, and we were thrilled to start a new chapter in our lives in a country we knew very little about. This was before the age of easy internet, and our access to information about the United Arab Emirates was limited to books and magazines. The skills I had learned early on as a child, of transplanting repeatedly, came in handy during this time. The learnings helped ease the transition and made the "new" feel comfortable quickly. After all, I knew that as long as I unpacked and settled the kitchen first, as I had seen my mom do, my roots would find their ground.

The decades of moving within India and then beyond, from Dubai to Toronto to Calgary and back again, with multiple stops in between, have all influenced my cooking and my kitchen today. Each new city taught me something new about food and how to cook, shop, and eat. Neighbours and friends, and conversations with shopkeepers in the *souq* (street market), all introduced me to new foods and techniques and how to incorporate them into everyday kitchen habits. This was also the time that I was noticing the differences, for example, between speedy chemically dried red chili powder and the slowly sun-dried version, or between small-batch spice blends made by a village collective and what was available in large international markets. All the moving and experiences around the world were helping me explore and experiment in the kitchen. And re-creating long-known family classics in my kitchen was another way I continued to connect to the life and people I had left behind.

My childhood and youth in India influenced me deeply, and while my kitchen in Canada today looks very different from my mother's in India, the principles I base my practices on are mostly grounded in what I learned from my family. Principles like creating a sense of abundance with what we have, even when what we have may be limited; reducing what we throw away because there may be another use for it; and, above all, never forgetting that the choices we make have an impact on the health and well-being of others as well as our own lives. These values that I inherited early on have guided me in my life, in my home, and in my kitchen, and they also form the foundation for this book.

IT WAS ALWAYS
ABOUT THE FOOD

I have always lived in the trenches with food, first during my nomadic years with my parents and brother, later with my husband, and then as a parent of two young kids. Thinking about how (and also what!) we cook and eat has always been a big part of my life. But those years of uprooting and transplanting took their toll.

As a gardener, I have learned how transplanting is hard on the plant's structure. Often the plant will go into shock. Leaves show the impact first; they start wilting, will drop off even, and the plant can lose a branch or two. But slowly, under the ground, with enough rich soil, air, water, and sun, the roots will start to recover, stretching, often unseen. Next, the stem will right itself and strengthen. The leaves return too, eventually, and the flowers take their time. After years of having my hands in the soil and also learning from my mom, I understand now that a transplanted shrub may not flower that first year. Due to root shock, as this period of transition is called in gardening, the shrub may not even flower the second year, but with enough care and support, in time the plant will recover and the blooms will return.

Root shock affects plants, and also humans. I am evidence of this theory.

My early motherhood years in Calgary, raising young kids and living on the opposite side of the world from all that was familiar, were difficult without the connection with my family. My husband and I juggled parenting responsibilities and busy careers. Slowly, we made new friends in the new city, and our united love for the outdoors drew us to explore the incredible Rocky Mountains as often as we could. Cooking at home took a back seat during those early years. For years afterwards, I cooked with my eyes closed. But because I had inherited my mom's palate and her skills, what I made in the kitchen tasted great.

The food and flavours were fantastic, but the connection with the food was missing.

We have moved many homes since the kids were born, and each time, just as I had as a child, we put away our kitchen crockery and cutlery first. Even when they were little, my kids knew that if the dinner plates and spice jars were unpacked, we were settled. And that first dinner? That was often at home, cobbled together from the pantry with canned chickpeas and pickled veggies, and eaten around an upside-down cardboard box.

STAYING ROOTED
BUT MOVING FORWARD

A few years ago, when we moved from Calgary back to Toronto, where I am as I write this book, I started collecting and sharing stories about real-life food and immigrant culture through my blog, *Maple and Marigold*. I was feeling the pull to slow down after kid number two and switch gears from my corporate marketing career. I started writing. What started as a love letter to my home in Canada (the maple in the blog's name) and my roots in India (the marigold), and a place to share my love of food in the kitchen is today helping people create positive change in their homes.

In the years after, through my continued learning, my expertise expanded. In 2020, during a long period of lockdown, I took the time to study the happy coincidence between food and mood. I learned that good food that feeds the body can also nourish the mind. As I went through the course material from Prof. Felice Jacka and the Food and Mood Centre at Deakin University in Australia,[1] I noticed an overlap, a delightful coincidence: the food that was best for our mood and mental health was also the best food we could choose for the long-term health of our planet. What we ate could save us, and the planet too!

The practices and principles I had been introduced to as a child in my parents' home and my mom's kitchen—practices like choosing what's best for us and for others, making do with what we have, and making it last—were bringing me full circle.

I love food. I love growing it and preparing it. For all the effort it takes, I love feeding it to friends and family too. I believe food is the bridge between people. My practices around food come from what I have learned, as well as the accumulated wisdom that has been passed down to me from my parents and the generations before them.

Along with my love for food, I also care about where it comes from, what goes into growing and raising it, and the journey that one delicious bite travels from farm to table. And, once that surprisingly resource-intensive, time-consuming journey is complete, I am someone who cares deeply about how the food that nourishes us becomes waste to end up in landfills around the world.

LOOKING TO THE FUTURE

We've known for a while now that eating the right kind of food will improve our physical health. But there is more: the right food can also improve our mental well-being through the two-way bridge that forms the gut-brain connection. What we eat feeds our bodies *and* our minds.

In this book I take this even further; research is showing us that our food and choices around the dinner table can also help save the planet.

The world has changed, incredibly, since I was that little girl walking through the market alleys along with my mom in Dehradun, India. In this book, I bring what I have learned, the science and generational wisdom together, to help people adopt a new way to cook, eat, and enjoy. I invite you to do the good work to reconnect with what you eat, without sacrificing the things we all love: flavour, plenty, and the grace to gather with loved ones.

What to Expect in This Book

Good Food, Healthy Planet is a celebration of good food, dishes that offer a feeling of plenty, even during times of constraint and shortages. Along with delicious flavours, you'll also discover robust, often overlooked ingredients that, my hope is, will inspire you to be creative in the kitchen. It's not about small steps and incremental change anymore; instead, we need giant leaps toward good-for-us, climate-conscious habits to help us all make the best of what we have. This book is written for people who work hard to sustain themselves and their families every single day, who are thinking beyond what's on their plate; it's not only about flavour and personal well-being, but also about the long-term impacts of what we cook and eat.

In 2019, a team of top scientists from around the world came together as part of the EAT-*Lancet* Commission on Food, Planet, Health[1] to investigate if a healthy diet could save the planet. The answer was a resounding "not if, but how."

The book that you hold in your hands translates the science from multiple sources, including recommendations from the planetary health diet created by EAT-*Lancet* and recent food and mood research.[2] Shaped by my Indian roots, it lays out what I have learned in practical, climate-conscious strategies, recipes, and tips designed to change the way you cook and eat every day.

At the core of the book lies an accessible and achievable framework that I cheekily call Eating with Benefits, a practical and ridiculously easy approach that keeps the health of people and the planet front and centre.

Past the framework, you will find kitchen stocking advice—what you need to have on hand to cook and eat in this new way, a way that I'm glad to share doesn't cost much and isn't overly complicated either. You'll see that I subscribe to the "power of less" principle even while stocking the kitchen. It's about affordable, planet-friendly ingredients, a short list of kitchen essentials, and easy-to-follow practices that work for real life.

The recipe collection is the final section of this book. I've kept them, just like the recipes on my website, mapleandmarigold.com, easy to customize. It's all about building delicious flavours with spices and ingredients, tried and tested recipes, and cooking creatively to double your veggies, love your lentils, boost your beans, swap out the meat, and more. You'll also find my quick hacks and tricks scattered throughout the pages, with recipe notes and #GoGreen tips to connect you to the food and to soothe confusion as much as possible.

Let this book be your guide. Once you have had a chance to read it, bring it back to your kitchen and store it in a drawer so it's always within reach. Let it catch some battle scars—a few oil splashes and a turmeric stain or two—then show these scars off with pride. For there's glory in home cooking. We're the unsung heroes of boring, mundane routines who fight a rigorous battle in the kitchen every day. And when the kitchen is clean and the dishwasher is loaded, we emerge from the kitchen, victorious.

A final note, while I have you. *Good Food, Healthy Planet* is aligned with the United Nations Sustainable Development Goals (SDGs).In 2015, all the UN member states agreed to 17 goals in total that were created as a "blueprint for peace and prosperity for people and the planet, now and into the future."[3] My work and this book align with the following three goals in particular:

My Cooking Tips

If you're anything like me, you're juggling family, career, and self simultaneously, all the time. There's a lot on your mind. And if you have young kids, backpacks end up on the floor and homework somehow finds its way into the junk drawer in the kitchen. Been there, done that!

When I'm in the kitchen, I usually have multiple hats on; mom, writer, occasional Instagrammer and everyday food waste warrior are just four that come to mind. I have experienced first-hand how creating delicious flavours can be hard. Add in the additional complexity of cross-cultural kitchen practices and the desire to make climate-smart choices, and it can all seem really overwhelming.

So, before we start cooking, here is some last-minute advice I have learned the hard way.

Less is more. You don't need many tools or appliances to make the food in this book. As you'll see in chapter 3, if it's a tool that serves only one purpose, like an avocado peeler or a garlic press, then it doesn't find a home in my kitchen drawer. A sharp knife for the former and a microplane or a mortar and pestle for the latter will do just fine, and these items can serve in other ways too.

The stove is your friend. Most days I cook in a pan of some sort, directly on the stove, and many of the recipes here offer the same direction. The one big tip for cooking on the stove is to stay vigilant. Foods cook differently, depending on how they were grown and raised and processed. They release moisture and sugars at different rates too. This affects the speed of cooking and the texture of the dish you'll end up with. All stoves are different as well. Some are efficient in heating up (like our induction stove) while others are slower to catch up. Watch for a change in smell, a puff of unexpected steam, or, more obviously, the beeping of the smoke alarm. Trust your nose and eyes. Anything, when cooked long enough, can burn. Full disclosure: I've burnt a pot while boiling *water*! So stay in the kitchen when you have a pan on the stove unless my recipe states that it's okay to walk away and forget about it—then you totally can!

Andaaze se. One of the concepts I have learned from my mother is a measurement style that is unique to family-style home cooking and is used to describe any step/ingredient while cooking. It's a vague, almost affectionate term that means "eyeball it." Andaaze se. Examine the food in the pan closely, and then add what you need. This vagueness used to bother me and I would try to translate it into precision. I have since learned that living and cooking in high resolution is overrated. A little bit of blurring around the edges is beautiful in its own way.

Measure in cups and cans, teaspoons and tablespoons. Many cookbooks offer exact measurements in grams and millilitres; you won't find those here, and here's why. If the recipe needs that high level of precision, in ingredients or cooking, it probably isn't one that you can adapt and tweak easily. As a result, it didn't make its way into this book. When I teach people how to cook, I show how they can make the dish their own and customize it to their family's taste and enjoyment.

Swap ingredients for what you have. Try alternatives, taste, and adjust the moisture and seasonings in the dish accordingly. Here are some swaps I make regularly:

- Cheese for nutritional yeast (excellent for those who are eating vegan and crave the cheesiness, nutritional yeast is also a shelf-stable food that has some unique fermented qualities)
- Peanuts for sunflower seeds
- Soy sauce and jarred condiments for mustard and orange chutney (see the recipes on pages 125 and 121)
- Spinach for Swiss chard and beet tops—the possibilities, I promise, are endless!

Choose food that's unpopular or hard to pronounce. If it was grown somewhere as food, you can eat it. Strangely-coloured carrots, hard-to-cook cuts of meat, and whole grains with names that have more vowels than you expect all offer creative cooking inspiration. A quick internet search and you may be surprised at how much natural flavour is in these unusual (to you) foods.

Use mostly olive oil or ghee for cooking. I grew up with peanut, coconut, mustard, and rice bran oil, but good-quality, affordable versions of these are harder to find where I am. So it's olive oil or ghee for me at home and in this book. Olive oil comes packed with unique nutritional benefits and has a lovely flavour that shines in many dishes. For all other cooking, I use ghee. Science keeps going back and forth on ghee; it's a saturated fat, after all, so doctors say it's not great for heart health. At the same time, this ancient cooking fat comes packed with deep flavour and immense nutritional benefits. My advice: use some ghee, not too much, and you'll find it goes further than you think.

Which ghee is right for me?

I prefer homemade ghee to any other kind, especially when my mom makes it. But if you don't have my mom (or perhaps yours) around to transform simple milk and cream into homemade deliciousness, choose a dairy company that is run by someone with roots in India (I may be a teensy bit biased here) who use local milk—whatever *local* means to you.

Tweak recipes with foods that are accessible, in season, and local to you. When local to you isn't possible, choose to support villages, farms, and farmers in another part of the world. Every day I use many ingredients that are not readily available where I am, such as millet, *hing* (asafetida), and makrut lime leaves, for starters. I have found grocery stores in Toronto that source these from collectives and small farms around the world.

Choose fewer potatoes, no wheat, and less rice when possible. Don't get me wrong; potatoes, whole grain wheat, and rice of any kind are healthy foods, and I have nothing against them. But we eat a lot of them in various forms all day, so in this book, you'll see I suggest we look for alternatives:

- Swap all-purpose wheat flour for nutritionally dense chickpea flour.
- Instead of potatoes, choose other tubers—sunchokes, sweet potatoes, and yams are widely available. Diversity on the plate is a wonderful thing; we'll talk more about how wonderful in chapter 2.
- Use whole grains instead of white rice. Millet, barley, spelt, quinoa, and amaranth are all strong contenders for rice alternatives in my kitchen.

When cooking vegetables and legumes, use fat. A big mistake that many of us make when cooking vegetables, lentils, and beans is to skimp on the fat. These good-for-us, good-for-the-planet foods need added fat to make their flavours really shine, especially if they are to compete with the likes of meat. Red meat and chicken, even eggs, come with their own fat content, so plant-forward dishes are immediately at a disadvantage in flavour. Add a tablespoon or two of fat to even the playing field, please!

Play around with bold (to you) spices, whole and ground. Try a new herb or two, and test flavours and textures to discover what you and your family like.

Finally, make the dishes your own! Adjust the recipes and cooking times to work with your kitchen habits, appliances, ingredients, and routine. Taste as you go along. Improvise to fit your life and your family's palate. Bring your culture and your family's food traditions into the mix.

What we cook and eat should reflect who we are and the times we live in. If you're like me, making a new life in a new country, discover new traditions around food. Fire up your creativity. The results may surprise you!

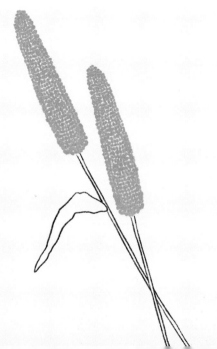

Chapter 1

The Big
Why

What's good food? I have been grappling with this question for a long time. It may have taken me a while, but I think I have finally cracked it.

Good food tastes good—great, even!

First of all, if a dish doesn't taste yummy, then it's out, right? Good food is first about flavour, but that's not enough. It also has to be good *for us*. Over decades, our knowledge about healthy food and its nutritional benefits has been evolving. It's about vitamins, minerals, proteins, fibre, and so much more. Researchers are finding out that good-for-us food is about more than just the micro- and macronutrients. What we eat affects our bodies and also our minds. Food affects our gut health, which influences our brains, our memory, and even our emotions.

So, what does this mean? Good food is tasty, and it also has a positive impact on our overall well-being, both physical and mental. But its effect doesn't just stop here. As it turns out, good food that is essential for our health is the same food that is good for the long-term health and prosperity of the planet. It's this last part that is the missing piece for so many of us. We begin with body because that's what we're most familiar with, but as you continue to read you'll see that it's only one tiny sliver of what we need to know, what is actually important. Let's explore this more.

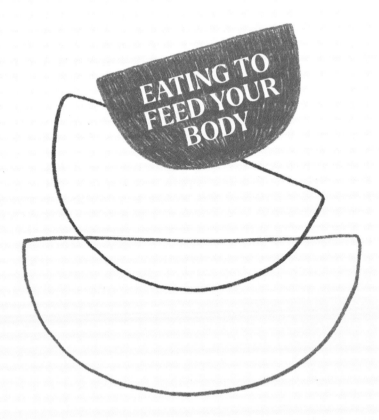

How Does What We Eat Affect Our Physical Health?

For decades, scientists have examined the impact of diet and nutrition on the human body. Their research concluded that poor diet is the leading cause of death in men and the second leading cause for women. Researchers analyzed slivers of nutrition and how they flowed through the human body, from our toes to our fingertips to the crowns of our heads, how they were absorbed, and their influence on how our bodies function and age.[1]

The evidence is clear. Food is fundamental for healthy bodies and to maintain our overall health and well-being. And yet there is more to this story. The emphasis on how food influences our physical health has shaped the lion's share of conversations around good food; food must be good for the body, we are told, to be counted as good food.

If the body is a well-oiled, well-functioning machine, then food is the fuel that makes it run. But we are more than well-oiled, well-functioning machines, and food is more than just fuel.

We have known for a long time that what we eat and our physical health are interconnected, but only recently have we widely acknowledged that what we eat affects our minds as well.

Can We Eat Our Way to Feeling Good?

A growing body of research around food's impact on our minds has tackled the question "Can we eat our way to feeling good?" The answer is, quite simply, yes! What we choose to cook with and eat feeds not only our bodies but also our minds. There exists a deep, two-way connection, called the gut-brain axis, between the belly and the brain that shows how the health of one directly affects the well-being of the other.[2]

This merits repeating: our gut health directly affects our mental well-being. So, going back to a question that has plagued so many of us, especially since the turbulence of 2020: "Can we eat our way to feeling good?" Yes, we can!

The world has changed a lot since the beginning of the global pandemic, and while its fallout is yet to be fully calculated, one thing is clear: people are struggling, and it's showing up in a variety of ways. In 2021 the United Nations announced that the mental health and well-being of communities around the world had been severely affected.[3] Since then, fear about the health impacts of COVID-19, worries for family, extended isolation, financial uncertainty, and the prospect of job loss have all been causing deep distress around the world.

Scientific research has revealed the deep, two-way connection between the gut and the brain, and how

EATING TO
FEED YOUR
BRAIN

the health of the gut's microbiota directly affects mental health. Recent research conducted at the Food and Mood Centre, with its SMILES Trial (a randomized, controlled trial that tested dietary intervention as a treatment strategy for depression)[4] and more, has determined the connection between diet, gut health, and mental health. The science is clear: we can improve our mental well-being if we consume a diet that is rich in whole grains, nuts and seeds, fruits and vegetables, fermented foods, eggs, beans, lentils, some fish, and even a tiny amount of meat.

This study and the research that followed on the impact of food on our minds, which includes mood, memory, and brain function, ran over multiple years, and while more work is being conducted on the topic around the world, here are some of the highlights I've discovered so far:

Our physical and mental health are closely linked. What we put in our bellies affects our gut microbiota, the millions and millions of microscopic organisms that live inside our digestive tracts. And because the gut and brain are connected via a bridge called the gut-brain axis, the gut microbiota controls the body *and* the brain.

- *Simply stated*: Our gut microbiota is crucial for our ability to survive and thrive, and these micro-organisms that live in our bellies directly influence our brain.
- *Bottom line*: A healthy gut is essential for our physical health and also our mental well-being.

Gut health supports brain plasticity. We need parts of our brain to grow and change continually so that we can continue to learn, remember, and feel. This is called brain plasticity, and one of the key ways we can support it is by eating more of the foods that reduce inflammation in the gut to support our brain health.

- *Simply stated*: A gut-poor diet increases inflammation in the gut, which adversely affects the brain.
- *Bottom line*: A diet rich in gut-healthy foods helps us think more and feel better.

The health of our gut is directly dependent on the quantity of our gut microbiota, and also its quality and diversity. The quality, quantity, and diversity of the food we eat influence the health of our gut microbiota. Good gut health plays a big part in our overall health, including our digestion, immunity, and in general, physical and mental health.

- *Simply stated*: Eating a diverse diet that's rich in gut-healthy foods improves the quantity, quality, and diversity of our gut microbiota.
- *Bottom line*: Diversity in what we eat helps our brains feel and function better.

There is more exciting and hopeful news. Research also indicates an approximate turnaround time. Changing diet can change the health of gut microbiota, sometimes quite quickly. This means making shifts in our diet and moving toward more gut-healthy foods will reduce inflammation, boost our immunity, and support brain function and that we see and, perhaps more importantly, feel the benefits quickly.

Great news, right? But there is more to this story than eating for good physical and mental health.

There has always been this notion that good food must be tasty *and* good for us. While that is true, defining good food in these self-centric terms is simply not adequate anymore. We should expect *more* from what we eat. Good food should improve us, our bodies and our minds, but it isn't enough unless we also prioritize the prosperity of the planet.

Can We Eat Our Way to a Healthier Planet?

For decades, we have known that food has an enormous impact on the planet. Agriculture causes 35 percent of the world's greenhouse gases, the main factors causing climate change.

In August 2019, the United Nations Intergovernmental Panel on Climate Change (IPCC) released a special report on food, agriculture, climate change, and land. This report, prepared by a group of 107 scientists from 52 countries, and subsequent reports since then, note that while food production practices were a major driver of climate change and source of greenhouse gases, food production is also the primary *victim* of climate change through impacts of sea-level rise, droughts, and flooding. This affects agriculture around the world.[5]

Our food systems feed the world, but the same systems in which we grow and raise food, and then cook, process, and eat it, is contributing to climate change. Having said that, climate change is forcing us to change how we grow, raise, and eat food. It's a vicious loop.

Along with other important findings, the IPCC report offered a comprehensive assessment of land use, and it noted that dramatic, immediate action[6] was needed to transform food systems around the world if humanity were to continue to thrive (see Notes and Recommended Reading, pages 258–260).

Around the same time this report was released, 37 top scientists from around the world came together for the EAT-*Lancet* Commission on Food, Planet, Health to investigate if a future population of 10 billion people could be fed a healthy, sustainable diet.[7]

The answer once again? A foot-stomping, resounding "not if, but how."

Let's look at all this scientific evidence again. In 2019, two major, global-level reports highlighted the enormous impact of greenhouse gas emissions from our food systems, agricultural land use, the loss of biodiversity, and the overuse of other crucial resources like water were having on climate change. The science was clear. These issues were the biggest threat to the planet. Since then, multiple reports by scientists worldwide have reinforced the urgency of this threat.

- *Simply stated*: Our food systems have an enormous impact on the long-term health of the planet.
- *Bottom line*: Transformation in our kitchen practices and eating habits is essential and could have an enormous positive impact on the planet. The time to make climate-smart choices is *now*.

> The planet is in crisis, but within this crisis we have our greatest opportunity. Because delightfully, coincidentally, the same food (well, mostly) that is good for us at a personal level is also good for the planet. That's legumes, whole grains, fermented foods, nuts and seeds, fruits and vegetables, which all utilize fewer planetary resources; add in some fish and eggs and tiny amounts of meat, and we are not only choosing foods that are healthy for our bodies and brains but also doing what we can for the prosperity of the planet.

EATING TO SAVE THE PLANET

"A diet that includes more plant-based foods and fewer animal source foods is healthy, sustainable, and good for both people and planet."
—EAT-*Lancet* Commission on a global planetary health diet, 2019[8]

Making the Case for People and the Planet

Our world is facing multiple crises that are converging simultaneously. There's the cost-of-living crisis, where a good standard of living is inching out of reach for many. The full extent of the mental health crisis is also being uncovered. Availability of food is another big issue: lineups at food banks are getting longer. And then there's climate chaos, which is often counted as one of the multiple crises but, in reality, affects all the others and is worsening already challenging situations.

Extreme events that used to occur once in a decade, like wild temperatures, landslides, droughts, and floods, have become commonplace. Add in accelerated biodiversity loss (more about this in the next chapter) and we're witnessing system-level disruptions around the world.

Nature is in big trouble. Humanity is in crisis mode. It's getting harder to produce, harvest, distribute, buy, and even cook food in the way we have always known. But there is good, hopeful news too, because when crises are multiple and interconnected, so are their solutions. That means even individual steps can go further to amplify collective impact.

Don't get me wrong; individual action isn't going to save us. We still need governments at all levels and corporations of all sizes to do their part to reverse the harm-causing practices and legislation that got us where we are today.

Having said that, individual action is where it all begins, with that first leap, which for so many of us starts with what we make for dinner.

- *Bottom line*: If you skimmed through this section, here's what you need to know. Healthy people depend on a healthy planet. The first doesn't thrive without the second. Good food is good for us, for our physical health and our mental well-being, only if it is good for the prosperity of the *planet*.

Let's expand the definition of good food to encompass not just us but everyone else. Good food is about flavour, enjoyment, and gathering, yes, *and* it is also about equity of resources and thinking about how we produce, what we consume, and how our choices affect the planet. This book is a long-overdue reset that busts archaic notions about "we've always done things this way" behaviour. It's about being realistic about where we stand at the crossroads of chaos and opportunity. Let's make the shift toward new practices and move forward with positivity and enjoyment, together.

EATING TO FEED YOUR BODY

EATING TO FEED YOUR BRAIN

EATING TO SAVE THE PLANET

Chapter 2

The Big
How

Good health and good food are deeply interconnected, we know this now. We have also learned about the impact our food systems have on climate change. The evidence is mounting. There's hard work ahead of us to slow down the worst and most widespread effects of climate-related chaos. To further complicate matters, it feels like everything is happening everywhere, all at once.

Our lives are interlinked, and recently we uncovered how deep-rooted this connection is when we saw with COVID-19 how what happens on one side of the world can quickly, directly affect the lives of billions on the other side of it.

While this may seem overwhelming, one thing is clear: if these disasters and crises are connected, so are the solutions. What you and I do today has a direct impact on how our lives turn out, and also on what happens on the other side of the world.

That's where Eating with Benefits comes in. A framework with a tongue-in-cheek name, it offers intentional and thoughtful actions that shift behaviour in the kitchen and also serve as a bridge between science and food. While it all starts with the people, there are no subtle steps to be found here, no incremental changes; now is the time for courageous leaps in the way we cook and eat. So here goes!

What Is Eating With Benefits?

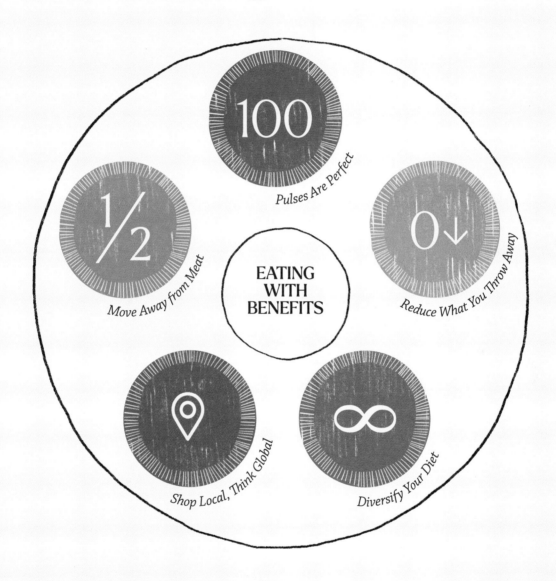

100

Pulses Are Perfect

1/2

Move Away from Meat

EATING
WITH
BENEFITS

0↓

Reduce What You Throw Away

Shop Local, Think Global

∞

Diversify Your Diet

Eating with Benefits is a framework that comprises five simple-to-follow principles that I've designed based on scientific research, traditional wisdom, and my own accumulated knowledge. The purpose of this framework is to help people cook delicious food while following good-for-us, climate-smart practices. It shows that while the science can be intricate and complicated, our food needn't be. There is tremendous change coming, and Eating with Benefits reveals all the practical, positive possibilities that lie ahead.

Diversify Your Diet

Let's start with what the dictionary has to say. *Diversity* is defined as "the condition of having or being composed of differing elements: variety," according to Merriam-Webster. There is more to this definition, of course, but in general, diversity of culture and thought, race and life experiences, all make living more interesting. I have believed in the value of diversity all my life, that it contributes to making our lives richer, more abundant, and above all more equitable.

Let's bring this back to the food. What about diversity on the plate?

Diversity in food can mean a few different things. For one, it's the representation of many cuisines on your plate. And if we consider food a gateway to culture, then multiple cuisines on a plate can represent diverse cultures, right? Food diversity can also mean a rich array of nutrients. This richness nurtures healthy gut microbiota, which in turn supports a healthy brain. We know from chapter 1 that good gut health influences good brain health because the quality, quantity, and *diversity* of our gut bacteria positively influence the brain. Following this logic further, a diverse plate leads to better overall health.

Unfortunately, the reality is that what we eat isn't diverse.

Eating a limited variety of foods has not only resulted in poor gut-health, it has led to the cultivation of more of the same crops around the world. Growing more of the *same* crops is bad news for a sustainable global food system because it sacrifices biodiversity.

FROM DIVERSITY TO BIODIVERSITY

Biodiversity is the variety of living organisms in the world. It is all the different kinds of plants and animals, fungi, and even micro-organisms that inhabit a particular area. Much like the gut microbiome—if you remember from chapter 1, these are the micro-organisms that live in our bellies—all organisms and species on the planet work together in intricate webs to maintain balance and support life. These living organisms are *everything* we need to survive and thrive, including fulfilling our most basic needs like food, clean water, shelter, and most medicines.

Did you know that 75 percent of the world's food supply comes from just 12 crops and 5 animal species? Or that in the Western world, we are currently eating fewer than 200 of more than 30,000 known edible plant species worldwide?[1]

Eat something different every day.

Slow Food International, a global, grassroots organization, describes biodiversity as "our insurance policy for the future, allowing plants and animals to adapt to climatic changes, attacks by parasites and disease, or the unexpected."[2]

But our collective ability to protect diverse animal and plant life is shaky at best; we are losing our planet's biodiversity at an alarming rate.

Science is clear. Increasing biodiversity in agriculture is critical to improving our collective health, reducing human impact on the environment, and helping us adapt to climate change.

- *Bottom line*: Eating a diverse, gut-healthy diet that's rich in foods that increase the quantity, quality, and diversity of our gut microbiota is good for our bellies and our brains. Additionally, as it turns out, an important part of supporting a healthier planet is expanding the variety of foods we eat and grow. Livestock, foods needed by animals, and very few crops have taken over land use, further limiting our biodiversity. This must change.

While this may feel a little complicated, here is some practical advice that works for real life.

HOW TO DIVERSIFY YOUR DIET

Try something different from the day before. If you eat spinach today, switch to arugula tomorrow. Ate broccoli yesterday? Choose Brussels sprouts today. New herbs and spices are also a great way to add diversity to your plate. Fresh is great, but dried works too.

Double your vegetable intake. Vote for biodiversity with a walk down the fresh aisles in your grocery store. With more than 30,000 known edible plants, let's bring some new ones home.

Eat more whole grains. Different ones, every day if possible. Whole grains are the most important food source for humans, but we are eating fewer and fewer servings of whole grains in general. Switching up our shopping and cooking routine and adding a variety of grains to our diet offers nutritional advantages and will also influence what's being planted around the world. Many alternatives to wheat, like millet, buckwheat, and quinoa are already readily available in smaller farming communities around the world.

Eat naturally fermented foods every day. The probiotics available in these foods enrich the belly and help us digest other foods. And with their sharp and tangy flavours, fermented foods add sparkle to every meal. Yogurt is a great way to add a probiotic-rich food;

pickled veggies are another easy option; drizzle some naturally-fermented soy sauce; set aside kombucha and *kanji* (an Indian fermented drink—recipe on page 135) to sip, and more!

Food diversity is a good place to start. But with the stakes so high and with the misconception that climate-smart solutions are expensive and cumbersome, it can all feel a little overwhelming. Despite the debate about the path we must follow to go green, the one thing most scientists agree on without a doubt is that we should *eat less meat*.

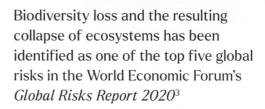

Biodiversity loss and the resulting collapse of ecosystems has been identified as one of the top five global risks in the World Economic Forum's *Global Risks Report 2020*[3]

"The difference in emissions between meat and plant production is stark— to produce 1 kg of wheat, 2.5 kg of greenhouse gases are emitted. A single kilo of beef, meanwhile, creates 70 kg of emissions."
—*Guardian*, September 2021[4]

"Beef is extremely inefficient to produce, as cattle consume a huge amount of calories and protein in order to produce a relatively small amount of calories and protein for human consumption (sheep and goat are similarly inefficient converters of feed to food, but are eaten on a much smaller scale globally). As a result, beef production requires large quantities of land and water per unit of protein or calorie consumed."
—World Resources Institute[5]

Move Away from Meat

By now you've probably heard that one of the best ways to be climate conscious is to stop eating meat, especially beef. But this can be challenging for those of us who love the flavour and texture of meat, and for some, it's even part of family traditions. So I understand some of the barriers to being vegan. In this section, I am going to show how we don't have to be vegan and give up meat entirely to make a difference. But what is clear is that we all need to cut our meat consumption way down.

Our food systems and agricultural practices cause 35 percent of total greenhouse gas (GHG) emissions, and meat is responsible for a whopping 60 percent of that total. In addition to GHG, roughly three-quarters of the world's farmland is used to pasture livestock, or to raise crops that feed livestock. Furthermore, an incredible quantity of freshwater resources are used in livestock farming, and what is left behind in farming communities and around animal feedlots is often irrevocably polluted.[4]

- *Simply stated*: The production of meat is a heavy burden on the planet. It causes tremendous GHG emissions, soil contamination, deforestation, and destruction of biodiversity. In addition, critical freshwater resources are being wasted especially in communities where dire shortages are already being predicted in the near future.

- *Bottom line*: Meat production and consumption cause enormous climate harm and are an inefficient way to use our dwindling resources. We need to shift our diet away from meat— beef, lamb, and mutton, in particular—to make a dent in our GHG emissions, conserve water, and direct land use to the growing of other crops. And eating too much meat is not great for our own health either.[6]

ALL FOR "SPECIAL" FOOD

For generations, red meat was considered a special food reserved for special occasions—*rogan josh* (slow-cooked curry) for when the extended family came over and a roast ham for a festive dinner. Over the last 40 years these traditions have undergone a shift; what was considered an occasional delicacy has become part of every day, every meal, mostly in its ultra-processed form.

This level of meat consumption is unsustainable, both for our own health and for our planet. But giving up meat entirely can feel unachievable, unattainable; fortunately, there is good news. Actually, two bits of good news!

First, initial findings from the food and mood research show that meat in very small quantities is good for our gut microbiome.[1]

Second, while veganism may be the most planet-friendly diet, I believe we don't need to go all the way to make a (big) difference. Progress is of paramount importance right now, and big leaping bounds of progress can be seen if we cut our meat consumption down.

The planetary health diet developed by the EAT-*Lancet* Commission on Food, Planet, Health recommends avoiding processed meat altogether and limiting red meat to no more than one serving per week. That's one serving smaller than the size of your palm, once a week. If this feels like a harsh target—I am struggling with it too—remember that eating *way* less meat, red meat in particular, can move us toward a more climate-conscious lifestyle.

While all these statistics are powerful, we need practical solutions to help us reduce our dependence on meat. Here are ideas to move away from meat.

Foods that cause the most GHGs around the world

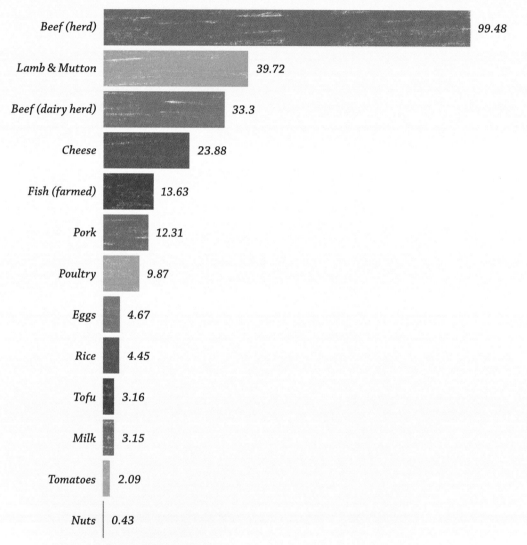

Food	Emissions
Beef (herd)	99.48
Lamb & Mutton	39.72
Beef (dairy herd)	33.3
Cheese	23.88
Fish (farmed)	13.63
Pork	12.31
Poultry	9.87
Eggs	4.67
Rice	4.45
Tofu	3.16
Milk	3.15
Tomatoes	2.09
Nuts	0.43

Emissions are measured in kilograms per kilogram of food produced (OurWorldinData.org).
Source: Poore, J., & Nemecek, T. (2018). Reducing food's environmental impacts through producers and consumers.

Halve the meat in your favourite meaty recipes. Swap it for other foods like mushrooms, green lentils, brown lentils, and oats.

Plan meals without meat. Choose plant-based options every day. Beans and lentils are great substitutes and can add flavour and texture. Many traditional cultures around the world, including some Indian communities, already eat vegan. A quick search on the internet will offer vegan recipe after recipe. You'll find cooking inspiration in this book too.

Adopt one or many of the latest meat-free trends. Like Veganuary or Vegan Curious, Meatless Mondays and Meat-free Wednesdays, Weekday Vegetarian, and Weekend Vegan. Try a flexitarian diet that includes meat or fish but occasionally. Embrace reducetarianism (see Recommended Reading, page 260), which reduces the amount of meat you consume. There are many ways to follow the same spirit of cutting out meat.

Swap out beef for other, more planet-friendly meats. Immediately. Frequently. As we know now, not all meat is equal. Beef (herd) and lamb have the highest carbon emissions among all types of meat and should be addressed for reduction immediately. While reducing our overall meat intake is a priority, poultry, chicken in particular, comes with a fraction of beef's carbon footprint and emissions.

If you're buying red meat, choose a cut that's unpopular, or what's left behind. Skip the steak for cheaper cuts. Unpopular cuts of meat like beef shank and pork collar are often available at cheaper prices. Cook them with robust, whole spices to bring out deeper flavours. See the recipe for Railway Beef Curry (page 217), which I make with stew meat or meat on the bone.

Consider the true cost of food. Pasture-raised beef is better for our health, for the animal, and for the planet, but the prices are usually higher. One way to avoid "sticker shock" at the grocery store is to remind ourselves that the price of grass-fed, organic, pasture-raised livestock often reflects the true cost of the food, a price that includes ethical, environmental, *and* health advantages.

I'll be frank: People don't like being told what to do, especially when eating meat is concerned. I have experienced a variety of very emotional responses on social media @MapleandMarigold and for that matter in person within my friends and family circles. When people love their favourite meat dishes, they find it hard (even impossible) to imagine a sumptuous meal without them. So, find what works for you and your family that will benefit the planet, too, and then dive in.

Once we have eased up on the meat in our diet, what's next? Well, if meat were to score a lowly 1 on the good-food scale, pulses would be a perfect 100.

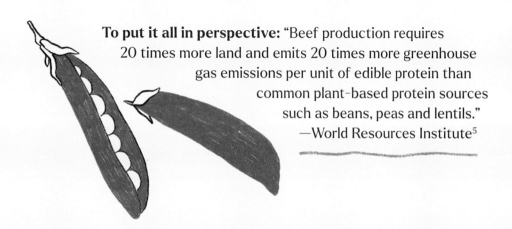

To put it all in perspective: "Beef production requires 20 times more land and emits 20 times more greenhouse gas emissions per unit of edible protein than common plant-based protein sources such as beans, peas and lentils."
—World Resources Institute[5]

Pulses Are Perfect

Pulses are the dried seeds of plants that include all the colourful and totally delicious beans, peas, and lentils. Many older cultures around the world are well known for their abundant varieties of bean-boosting, lentil-forward dishes. In northern India, for example, no meal is considered complete without a bowl of *daal* on the side.

Ranking up there for their affordability, flavour, and planet-friendly qualities, pulses are fantastic in many ways. They have a long and rich history of nourishing communities around the world, come naturally packed with protein and fibre, and are low in fat. Beyond their nutritional benefits, pulses are also easy to grow. They need less—or, dare I say it, no—human intervention, very little fertilizer, and use far less water vs. other crops. Legumes (another word for pulses) are able to draw nitrogen from the air and then fix it to help enrich the soil. You read that right! Pulses are self-sufficient enough to assess the needs of the soil and then fertilize it themselves!

Dried pulses are also shelf stable, so on Thursday when you're tired and the kids are hungry, there's always that bag of lentils hiding in the back of your pantry standing by to be transformed into a soothing and comforting bowl of goodness.

- *Simply stated*: Beans, lentils, dried peas, and pulses in general are great for our personal health, for soil and water health, and for the long-term prosperity of the planet.
- *Bottom line*: Swapping in these nutritional and environmental superheroes is not only an ecologically sound decision but also the cheaper, healthier, delicious choice.

Canned, fresh, or dried pulses in all their glory are excellent people- and planet-friendly food. They come in dozens of variations and colours with their own flavour and texture. If you like mild or mellow flavours, or earthy, robust, or even chewy and meaty, I promise there's a legume that's right for you.

One would think, with all the benefits, people would be lining up to fill their bowls with daal. Sadly, pulses often get a bad rap: people think they're hard to digest, difficult to cook, and, in many communities, they are considered a "poor people's food." So, what can we do to eat more pulses every day?

HOW TO ADD PULSES TO YOUR DAILY DIET

Buy, cook, and eat more legumes. In doing so, we start a people- and planet-friendly ripple that will ease the burden on our wallets, improve our health, and create a demand that will encourage farmers to grow more of these plant-based protein powerhouses. Growing more legumes regenerates soil and eventually makes farming easier. Costs of farming go down. Lower farming costs lead to higher land use toward growing beans and lentils, crops that we know use less water and resources. I am over-simplifying here, but you get the general idea, right? A small decision like choosing chickpeas for dinner can start a cycle that leads to reducing the adverse environmental impacts of agriculture and helps build a healthier future for all of us!

Here are some more ways to add more legumes.

Swap half the meat for lentils. Brown, French, Puy, and green lentils all have a texture and chewiness that matches that of meat really well in many recipes.

Keep canned beans, lentils, and peas on hand. They make a great last-minute meal, add robust texture and flavour to dishes, and can be stored in your pantry for years.

Try a new, perhaps unfamiliar, lentil recipe. Cultures around the world cook beans and lentils in wonderful and delicious ways. Cross-cultural dishes may also use new (to you) herbs and spices, making them great for boosting diversity on the plate too.

For generations, grandmas in India have been telling kids, "Finish your daal. It's good for you." As it turns out, they were right all along. And perhaps that bowl of daal can really save the world.

> Love your lentils (and lentils will love you right back).

What about faux meat as an alternative to regular meat?
I believe the perfect alternative to meat already exists. Mark Bittman, a renowned food author, describes this so well in his newsletter, so I will borrow his words: "It's funny, in a way, because the perfect meat alternative exists, and has always existed. It's natural, delicious, sustainable, even soil-boosting! It takes no research dollars and is the world's most important protein source. It's called the legume. Sure, it's not smoked brisket or a juicy burger, but it has fed cultures for centuries"[6]

Reduce What You Throw Away

Along with eating a diverse variety of food, cutting out meat, and eating way more pulses and produce, reducing our waste is the next big choice we can make to scale back on our environmental footprint.

Food waste is the single biggest component of trash in our landfills. And the problem is worse in Canada and the United States vs. most other countries.

The statistics on food waste are quite startling: Approximately 58 percent of the food produced in Canada and the United States is discarded.[7] This wasted food alone is responsible for roughly 8 to 10 percent of global greenhouse gas emissions[8] and approximately 38 percent of the total energy usage within global food systems.[9] Moreover, an estimated 28 percent of the world's agricultural area is dedicated to producing food that ultimately goes to waste.[10]

IT'S MORE THAN JUST A TOMATO

When we toss mouldy tomatoes or a half-eaten burger into the trash, we're wasting food, yes, but also throwing away the water, soil, and energy resources that were used to produce that food. We may see the discarded food and the resulting mountain of trash. We may even worry about methane, a powerful greenhouse gas that is emitted as the food breaks down. What may not be as evident is the enormous resource waste related to growing, raising, processing, transporting, stocking, cooking, and then throwing away the food.

There is more than enough food in the world to feed everyone, yet more than 826 million people go to bed hungry every night. This number continues to increase as the effects of the global pandemic ripple around the world.

According to the EAT-*Lancet* Commission's 2019 report, we cannot achieve a sustainable food system without addressing the challenge of food loss and waste.

- *Simply stated*: We throw away a disgustingly large amount of food. In Canada and the United States, that's more than half the food that we grow and produce.
- *Bottom line*: It's not all doom and gloom, though! Addressing this catastrophe of food waste is within our grasp, and it's even easier than some of our other challenges. Reducing what we throw away saves money, lowers our GHG emissions, eases the burden on landfills, and moves us many giant steps forward in the battle against climate chaos.

Like the other issues that affect people and the planet, this problem needs enormous corporate will and legislative intervention. In this book, we discuss the individual actions we can take in our kitchens and homes, individual steps that I'm pleased to report can accomplish a lot.

> We are what we eat, and we are also what we waste.

HOW TO REDUCE FOOD WASTE

Long before social media showed us low-waste kitchen hacks, ingenious grandmas around the world were cooking nose to tail, root to seed, with rinds, peels, leaves, tips, tops, and all.

You will find many recipes here that follow these back-to-basics practices that reduce waste, extend the life of food, and also save us money. My intent here is to show off the boundless possibilities that come with this way of cooking while applying the spirit of low- and no-waste living.

Choose what's imperfect and wonky first. Over years, supermarkets have shifted our perception toward perfect-looking produce. Many large chains even have uniformity standards of how fruits and vegetables should look. Admittedly, that's partly our fault because as consumers we tend to reach for what looks like what we imagine is a top-quality fruit, one with perfect shape and colour. The blemished tomato and twisty carrot often don't make the cut, right? So let's change that.

Buy only what you need. I found this to be the hardest because it's so easy to overbuy when you see a great sale, right? That enormous bag of peppers looks tempting, but by adhering to this step, we ease all else that follows.

Limiting our purchasing to only what we need means the market demand will reflect *real* consumption levels, not what's thrown away. Supermarkets will stock only what's needed. Food suppliers will use their tools to forecast more accurately, and they will supply the right quantities to meet that demand. Trucks that drive around from farm to plant will pick up only what is to be consumed. Refrigerators will store food, not waste-to-be. Packaging, storage, and delivery needs will cover actual demand, not what ends up in landfills.

Buying only what we need can eventually streamline the entire market process of harvesting, storing, distributing, and cooking food. It will close the loop on food waste.

If you do end up buying more than you need, bulk cook and freeze. Bulk cooking uses less energy per unit. And freezing what we don't need buys us time and will help the food last longer.

Finally, eat your leftovers. Box and label them, and stack them in the fridge by date. Reach for them when the temptation to order takeout is high. Remind yourself that you did the work already, and now it's time to enjoy the fruits of your labour.

Bought too many peppers and tomatoes this month?
Cook them down and make a sauce. Or start a communal cooking club where friends (or strangers) can get together to cook large batches of sauces and chutneys. Share the bounty and make new friends.

Try something new. What about those strange-looking bulbs at the farmers' market—kohlrabi—that look so intimidating? They make the best fritters or can be added to a stir-fry. Growing peas on your balcony? Did you know that it's not just the peas but also the shoots, tips, and leaves that are edible—and delicious?

Use all parts of the fruit and veg. You likely know beets roast up deliciously in the oven, but what about the beet tops that turn delicious when they're quickly sautéed in olive oil and garlic? Orange peels, potato skins, broccoli stalks, watermelon rinds—the odds and ends of fruits and veggies are not only edible but, with a little bit of care, also delicious.

Along with food, water is precious. Reuse the water that has been used to wash your whole grains and legumes. Store it in Mason jars for up to four weeks and use to water your backyard or houseplants.

Read up on dates. Expiration, best-before (BB), and sell-by dates are different things and can be confusing.
- Expiration is the date past which the food is no longer deemed safe to eat.
- BB is the date past which the food drops in quality of texture but is likely still safe to eat.
- Sell-by dates are for the stores, so that they know how long they can leave the food up on their shelves.

Generally, in my opinion, most food is safe to eat as long as there is no evidence of spoilage, such as visible mould or an off smell. Many processed foods are made with preservatives, designed to make the food last way longer than needed. Short expiration dates on naturally fermented foods like cheeses, yogurts, and pickles make little sense. After all, the purpose of fermentation is to extend the life of foods and to store them long-term. (Please note that this information is based on my common-sense approach and experience. Use this advice responsibly and judiciously.)

Grow some food. It doesn't have to be a whole backyard or an orchard. Just grow something; it will offer a new appreciation of how much effort, time, and patience one needs to grow a handful of tomatoes.

No backyard? Start with a cup or two of water on your windowsill and use it to regrow green onions, mint, and basil. Watch leftover bits regenerate into fresh food.

No space at home? Find a local community garden. Getting outdoors, meeting like-minded people, and growing some food at the end of it all is pure joy!

Compost at home. Make soil with the food waste that is left behind. Buy a pail, place it in your balcony or backyard, and use it to collect leftover vegetable trimmings and skins. After a week, throw the squelchy bits in your garden around your plants. That's it. Of course, you could buy equipment and kits for composting, but this here is the most basic way to compost, and in the end, you will have rebuilt the soil in your backyard. No backyard? Start by drying orange peels, tea leaves, and eggshells on your windowsill. Blend them and then store the mix in airtight bags. Sprinkle it around the base of the plant, and water as usual.

What we throw away is changing the planet in an awful way. Those wilted greens you found in the back of your fridge may not look so tasty, but choosing them for tonight's dinner matters.

Set aside fruit and veggie trimmings, corncobs, and all matter of husks to make:

Scrappy Stock (page 81)

Scraptastic Orange Peel Chutney (page 121)

No-Waste Watermelon Rind Curry (page 211)

What Your Food Comes Wrapped In

Is there anything sillier than peeled oranges tightly wrapped between plastic and Styrofoam? Or single bananas in cling film? Along with food waste, a big part of what ends up in landfills is the plastic packaging that comes with our food.

The invention of plastic changed the world; it made us safer, healthier, and, through the transformation of hygiene and cleanliness, less likely to die. But this innovative material was not designed to be disposable, used once and then discarded.

Nine percent of plastic around the world is recycled. Let's read that again. Only 9 percent of the plastic ever produced around the world has been recycled. Twelve percent has been incinerated, and the remaining 79 percent has ended up either in landfills or in nature, broken down by salt and sunlight into smaller and smaller pieces. These microplastics are being found in water, oceans, and soil. Recent research has found microplastics in people's lungs.[11]

The extravagant use of plastic around the world is causing devastating human and environmental hazards; it's infiltrating ecosystems and endangering biodiversity. Moreover, the production and disposal of plastic is contributing to GHG emissions and causing the depletion of natural resources.

What is even more alarming is that a significant amount of plastic being used today is avoidable. Plastic use is rising sharply even in a time when planet-friendly alternatives are being used and discovered every day. So what can we do to reel back this catastrophe?

HOW TO BREAK UP WITH SINGLE-USE PLASTIC

Use what you have. Run it into the ground, and when you need it again, bring in the non-plastic version.

Cut out plastic in your kitchen and at home. Buy foods that don't use plastic in their packaging, processing, and production. Learn about and use planet-friendly alternatives.

Support stores and businesses that follow low-waste principles. It's hard enough to be a small-business owner in the times we live in, harder still when you're advocating that consumers go low waste.

Break.
Up.
With.
Plastic.

Shop Local,
Think Global

First, the bad news. Buying food that's local to you isn't automatically better for the planet. How food is grown or raised, produced, and delivered to our kitchens can have more impact on GHG emissions than the "where," the geographic location. For example, greenhouse-grown, vine-ripened tomatoes may use a lot of energy through the long Canadian winters and may be less environmentally sound than sustainably grown tomatoes shipped from Mexico by train.

Now for the good news. Many small-scale businesses and farms nurture local communities and economies and are often respectful of local culture and traditions. Heirloom tomatoes and carrots and forgotten grains would remain forgotten if it weren't for work done by cooperatives and local farmers' markets. Shopping local and supporting local farms in turn supports smaller ecosystems and biodiversity within the area. These are important factors that bring people and the planet together.

There's more. Growing food closer to home makes us more resilient to supply chain issues. Russia's war with Ukraine is a good example that revealed the importance of a strong supply chain to the world. When Ukraine was invaded and Ukrainians were called to defend, regional farming and transportation, along with other systems within the country, came to a halt. Wheat and sunflower crops (and more) were abandoned and shiploads of food were stuck at east European harbours for months. Worldwide shortages ensued. The price of foods like pasta and noodles skyrocketed. Sunflower oil became harder to find, and as a result processed foods that used this key ingredient became more costly. This impact was felt most by developing nations where hunger and food insecurity were already high. Instant noodles were among the first to see the impact of this shortage; newspaper headlines in Indonesia told the story of noodle scarcity caused by supply chain disruptions as a result of events on the ground in Kyiv, 10,000 kilometres away.[12]

Finally, governments around the world started to see the advantages of growing food in their own countries, and of supporting local farming communities.

So what can we do to adopt shopping locally? As with everything else, a lot!

Buy what's made, grown, and processed locally as much as possible. When that isn't possible, shop at smaller stores and neighbourhood markets. Support local endeavours in freecycling, upcycling, reusing, and sharing resources.

Eat what's in season where you live. This is understandably hard, especially living in Canada, as I do, where the produce growing season is short. But climate change and supply chain challenges have permanently changed our buying behaviour, our food systems, and how affordable food is (or isn't) around the world. Synchronizing our kitchens with the seasons as much as possible helps us not only deepen our connection with food it also helps us eat in a healthy, planet-friendly way.

Talk to shopkeepers and small-business owners about their obstacles. Jim, whom I mentioned earlier, runs our local fruit market and is a small-business owner. In talking to him about frozen strawberries, I found out that wholesale fruit and veggie suppliers offer easier purchase terms and returns to larger supermarkets. These supermarkets may even receive a credit on produce that deteriorates faster, like greens and fresh berries. These returns—the wilted produce—often end up in the landfill. So, while offering easier returns and concessions to larger supermarkets may be a good business strategy for food distributors, it has a negative financial impact on smaller, neighbourhood markets that have to work harder to limit food waste in their businesses. Poor strategy for people and the planet.

The principles of Eating with Benefits are designed to take us beyond the science of food and connect us to the land, to truly see where our food comes from. I hope these strategies help you simplify healthy climate-conscious cooking at home and steer people away from unhealthy, unsustainable, unaffordable practices.

With so much out of our control, isn't it wonderful that we can chip away at a problem as enormous as climate change by doing something as simple as shifting what we eat for dinner?

There's a notion out there that shopping and eating local is more expensive. And yes, looking at our grocery receipts, in the short term, that may be correct. In the long run though, taking into account true cost accounting principles that include the social, human, and natural costs of food production, distribution, consumption, and disposal, shopping local doesn't hit the wallet hard at all.

What is true cost accounting (TCA)?
This is a holistic accounting approach that states that the cost of a product or service should reflect its true cost to society. It considers and makes visible the social, environmental, and economic impacts of the production of a good or service, from the extraction of raw materials to the end-of-life disposal of the product and all related items. TCA recognizes that businesses often pass the costs of their product's life cycle on to society and instead works to create a more equitable and sustainable economy. For example, a 12-pack of bottled water is often sold for less than $3, a price that does not reflect the heavy costs of production of the plastic bottles and the end-of-life disposal of plastic.[13]

Dispelling False Notions

There is a lot of misinformation and misconceptions about food, planet-friendly food in particular. The reality is, we simply cannot continue to shop, cook, and eat the way we have. To ease this transition, let's tackle some of these false notions.

It needs to be all or nothing. There's often a debate over whether our modifications need to go all the way to make an actual difference. I believe all changes that are made with the interests of both people and the planet in mind are meaningful. Don't let perfect be the enemy of good.

Climate-friendly cooking is complicated and time-consuming. This is simply not true. Shifting to any new routine in the kitchen is cumbersome, but cooking sustainably? That's easy once you know how! The proof is in the recipe collection at the end of this book, where perhaps the most time-intensive recipe, Railway Beef Curry (page 217), is also the least climate smart.

Eating for the planet is expensive, especially in the times we face today. Again, not true. Beans and lentils are some of the world's cheapest and most nutritious foods, and they are available in almost every corner of the world. Current research points to how growing and eating beans and lentils in the short term can actually save the world in the long term.[14] Furthermore, the economics of food (and most everything else) have been figured out only for the short term. Cheap food is misleading in itself. After all, we are still calculating the effects of the food's production and consumption on the whole system. Expanding the use of true cost accounting principles, it is clear that we don't have another choice. We can't afford to cook and eat any other way.

Fish is sustainable. Fish makes a healthy, delicious meal. Good for people, yes, but as far as the planet is concerned, we are causing great harm to our oceans, rivers, and waterways with our fishing practices. Fishing has changed over the decades. It's no longer someone at the end of a fishing rod out for a day on a boat. It's much more likely that our seafood has been caught by a major operation that is fishing far into the ocean in ways that are destructive to ocean life. So consider this when you're buying seafood:

- Where was the fish caught? Buy local, whatever local means to you.
- If you can't buy local, buy from a locally run store. You're supporting a small business, and the fishmonger will be open to chatting about the store's sustainable seafood list.
- Be flexible when you're out shopping for your meal plans. Locally caught haddock not available? Buy sole or cod or another fish. (See Recommended Reading, page 260, for tips on buying sustainable seafood.)

Organic produce is best. Yes and no! Traditional Indian knowledge recommends we choose organic food as much as possible because these foods use no (or fewer, depending on where you live) pesticides or fertilizers. This is better for our health and for the planet. From the perspective of the environment, this lower use of fertilizers and pesticides results in less runoff, so it encourages a wider variety of plants for biodiversity. Organic farming in general results in better soil health and lower levels of water and land pollution. So it would seem organic food is better for the planet, right? Except that the answer isn't so clear. Recent studies show that GHG emissions are far higher on large farms that follow organic practices, and the entire process, for many reasons, is still taxing on the soil and on the environment. So here's my common-sense approach when I'm considering organic:

- Choose organic when buying fresh produce that will be eaten raw, with the skin on.
- Choose organic meat and dairy, because animals in organic environments, in general, are treated with more care.
- Choose regenerative farming methods or initiatives that support agroecology, a more holistic approach that balances science with social and political justice. When neither is available, support small farms and farmers.
- Finally, what we eat has more impact than how it was grown and raised, so continue to choose mostly beans, legumes, whole grains, fruits and veggies, some dairy and fish, and small amounts of meat.[15, 16]

Soil is everything.
"Did you know 95% of the planet's food is grown on a few cm of topsoil, that is being degraded at an unprecedented rate?" Fortunately, topsoil is a renewable resource, and one key way to renew it is through compost.
—Food and Agriculture Organization of the United Nations[17]

What is possible if we swap out just one hamburger?
A study by Tulane University notes that if "Americans swapped one serving of beef per day for chicken, their diets' greenhouse gas emissions would fall by an average of 48 percent and water-use impact by 30 percent."[18] That's a world of possibilities right there.

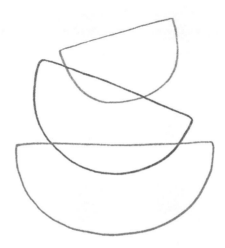

In the battle against food waste, meat doesn't get a pass.
Meat is a highly resource-intensive food. Its production causes GHG emissions, uses and pollutes enormous quantities of water, and harms soil health so nothing can grow in the area again. And yet one US statistic states that 28 percent of meat ends up being thrown away. So what can we do? Reduce our meat intake, for one, buy only what can be eaten immediately, and then freeze what we can't eat right away.

Beef is the most emissions-intensive food.
According to a landmark study, every kilogram of beef consumed adds a whopping 99.5 kgs of CO_2 equivalent greenhouse gases to the environment, on average. It was the most climate-damaging food studied, and the competition wasn't even close.[19]
—*Guardian*, May 2023

Chapter 3

How to Stock a Good Food Kitchen

If you've ever gone down a rabbit hole watching late-night videos on the latest kitchen hacks, you know navigating the world of cooking healthy and delicious food can be confusing. Add in the extra complication that people may assume comes with climate-conscious habits, and it can feel like cooking good food takes more time and effort than we can afford at this time, right?

In this section, I offer all the practical and possible ways to ease into new routines that work not only for you and your family but also for the planet.

While abundance and plenty lie at the heart of this book, here I show how it's actually subtraction that will truly transform our habits. Cooking more, better and more deliciously, is all possible . . . with less.

The advice and lists in this section are based on the core principles of Eating with Benefits They have been compiled based on what I have learned over the years. This is not meant to be an exhaustive list; you may not even see many of the usual suspects you are accustomed to in your everyday routine. My purpose here is to encourage people to use what they have and reduce what is thrown away. To that end, I cover basic tools and foods that most home cooks will need in order to prepare a wide variety of people- and planet-friendly meals.

Chances are there will be items that you and I don't agree on. I remember how a discussion on the value of a knife block and set turned passionate on Instagram a while back. In case you're wondering, I don't have a block and don't plan to get a set, ever. I would rather buy a chef's knife from one maker and a paring knife from another that works for me and the angle at which I hold the knife. Same goes for cookware. I have a pair of mismatched skillets, a small *tadka* tempering frying pan, a medium-sized *tawa* roti pan, and a Dutch oven that match with nothing else—nor with each other.

Here is a list of things that ease the act of cooking in my kitchen. I hope they do the same for you.

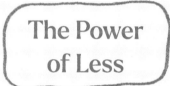

Kitchen "Essentials"

After uprooting and transplanting numerous times—14 cities before I turned 18, and 7 since then—the one constant was always the kitchen. And while I always understood the importance of cooking at home, the cabinets were often sparsely stocked. In some apartments, we were limited by storage space; in others, it was knowing that the need to uproot might come sooner than expected.

While I list many of the following items as "essential" pieces of kitchen equipment, if I am honest, you don't really *need* most of them. With just a paring knife, a pan, a mortar and pestle, and a heat source, you can make a variety of delicious meals that still adhere to the principles of Eating with Benefits. With that in mind, here goes!

FIVE SMALL APPLIANCES

- Blender
- Small spice grinder
- Immersion blender
- Mini chopper, or, if you have enough storage space, a food processor
- Pressure cooker (Instant Pot)

A pressure cooker will change the way you cook lentils, beans, whole grains, and meat. While the stovetop is great, an electric pressure cooker offers hands-free, worry-free cooking. Pressure cooking, in general, uses less energy and water than most other cooking techniques, and it doesn't heat up the kitchen quite as much as the stovetop or oven. A great option when you're trying to keep cool.

> Buy the stuff that works for you. Make it last. Run it into the ground.

COOKWARE

- Three heavy-bottomed pots/saucepans of various sizes (small, medium, large, one each), some with lids
- One small heavy-bottomed pan that works for tadka (cast iron or stainless steel is best)
- Two heavy-bottomed skillets of different sizes (6, 8, or 10-inch are most popular) appropriate for stovetop and oven use. Choose the smaller sizes when you're cooking for 4 people or less.
- Ceramic, clay, cast iron, or glass baking dishes (a mix of materials work across multiple functions)
- A universal flat lid that works for pans without lids
- At least one baking sheet and a couple of baking pans/dishes for roasting, baking, and grilling

Try your local thrift store for baking dishes. Over the years, I have discovered a great many around Toronto.

#GOGREEN TIP: Boiling water for eggs? Place the lid on the saucepan. This traps the heat inside the pot so less energy is needed to heat the water.

UTENSILS AND OTHER TOOLS

- Two sharp knives for paring, chopping, slicing, and dicing
- One medium serrated knife for thicker-skinned vegetables like tomatoes (the same knife works for bread)
- Two cutting boards, one for meat/dairy and one for non-meat items (glass and ceramic are my favourites)
- Measuring cups and spoons, various sizes
- Small, medium, and large mixing bowls for washing, rinsing, blending, mixing, sprouting, and all sorts of multi-tasking
- A whisk or two
- A peeler, with corer
- A colander for draining pasta and washing veggies and fruit
- A mesh strainer for straining lentils, yogurt, and paneer
- A wooden spatula or two, tongs, a rice paddle, and a soup ladle that does double duty as a curry ladle
- A grater, with large and small holes
- A mortar and pestle

STORAGE AND REUSABLES DRAWER

- Clear glass storage containers of different sizes, with lids. These are great for storing leftovers, meal prep, and cooked grains, beans, and lentils. Look for options that are fridge and freezer friendly, and also microwaveable.
- Beeswax wraps
- Silicone baking mats
- Glass jars of varying sizes, with lids. Upcycle tomato sauce, pickle, and jam jars. Real life rarely matches, so your pantry jars needn't. The variety also indicates that you have done the work to rescue and repurpose. You're a low-waste warrior. Accept the glory!

- Small plates of all sizes to use as lids and for prep
- Cotton bags with drawstring for storing, sprouting, and soaking
- Tea towels, of various sizes and fabric weights
- Washable wipes for kitchen cleanups

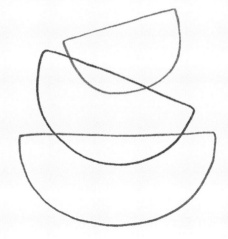

Buy multiple large sheets of beeswax wrap instead of cling-film. Trim the sheets down to fit the bowls you use in your kitchen. Wash with warm water and soap as needed. Beeswax wraps not as clingy anymore? Revive by heating for 2–3 minutes in the oven. Set the temperature at the lowest setting (50–75°F) and allow the beeswax to soften again. Take the wrap out and hold by the corners to cool.

#GOGREEN TIP: Reuse aluminum foil. Wipe it down or wash to remove sticky food residue. You can even wash foil in the dishwasher, top drawer only. Dry and store to use another day.

Swap out single-use parchment paper with long-lasting, washable silicone baking mats. Go one step further and use the baking sheet or pan "naked." To clean, apply a paste of baking soda, then heat through and scrub gently.

Sticky label on a jar? Soak the jar in hot water for 30 minutes. Scrape the label away with a knife. If the glue residue remains, massage in a drop or two of vegetable oil, let it sit for a few minutes, and then scrub with soap and a scrubber as you would normally.

#GOGREEN TIP: Tea towels looking worn out? Cut them into 6 × 6-inch pieces, fold them, and set them aside. Use instead of paper towels for exceptionally dirty messes. Do the same with old cotton T-shirts.

Pantry Staples

A well-stocked pantry protects against all manner of shortages and supply chain disruptions. So many of us learned this lesson during those early months of the pandemic. A well-stocked pantry is also a buffer that helps people plan for future dinners amidst uncertainty or price fluctuations. Having said that, I wouldn't recommend stocking every (or even most) ingredient you feel you may need in the future. Plans change; even shelf-stable, long-life food will rot before we can get to it all.

Aside from a few spices and other items, most ingredients you need for the recipes in this book are fairly straightforward and widely available in many large, city grocery stores. If there is an odd ingredient that proves difficult to find, try a multicultural market or an Indian/Asian grocery store close to you.

#GOGREEN TIP: Buy pantry staples loose and in bulk, if you have the space. Dried lentils and beans in their whole form can be stored for years in the pantry. Whole spices and grains will last for a long time too.

Buying in bulk saves money and packaging. Decant the food into glass jars, and leave a card inside with the name of the food and the month/year of purchase. Unlike stickers, this card can be swapped out easily when the jar is empty.

WHOLE GRAINS

Grains are the seeds of plants that belong to the grass family. Whole grains are those that have not been refined and thus contain all the edible parts of the seed, including bran, endosperm, and germ. This makes them much more nutritious for our personal health, and as it turns out, eating a variety of unprocessed grains is also great for the health of the planet.

Whole grains can be stored for a long time (think years) in the pantry till they start to smell off. That's when the oils in the grains will have turned rancid and it's time to compost.

Here are some of my favourite whole grains. Some items in this list are technically pseudocereals that behave and can be treated like whole grains:

- Amaranth
- Barley—purple and pot
- Buckwheat
- Bulgur
- Corn—whole grain cornmeal and polenta
- Farro
- Millet—finger, pearl, and white
- Oats—steel-cut and rolled
- Quinoa
- Rice—brown and white, short- and long-grain
- Sorghum
- Spelt
- Teff
- Wheat—kernels, cracked, and wheat berries

Try a forgotten grain or two: These are any number of whole grains that were used in ancient cultures that have become less popular over the last few decades: for example, millet, spelt, barley, farro, sorghum, and teff, among many others. Forgotten grains are considered nutritionally superior to the more commonly consumed grains like wheat and rice, as they are typically higher in fibre, vitamins, and minerals. Bringing them back into everyday eating promotes agricultural diversity too!

FLOURS

While flour made from wheat is most widely used and commonly available, all grains, forgotten and otherwise, can be bought in flour form. Bean and lentil flours are great options for both flavour and health benefits. Look for words like *stone-ground*, *whole grain*, and *wholemeal* on the package label.

Four flours that you will always find in my pantry:

- Wheat flours—whole grain and whole wheat, occasionally all-purpose. These are often used for baking.
- Atta—this is wholemeal flour where all the layers of the wheat kernel have been milled together to form a slightly grainier flour. It is often a very pale brown colour and different from wholewheat flour. Atta flour is used for chapatti (page 99)
- Rice flour—used as a thickener and to make batter and fritters crispier
- Chickpea flour—also known as gram flour or besan

NUTS AND SEEDS

Nuts and seeds are nutrition powerhouses. While whole and unprocessed nuts are popular, nut milk consumption is trending too. We are going nuts for nuts right now.

Some nuts (listed as "occasionally choose" below) are resource intensive but fit within the Eating with Benefits principles because of how they support local farming communities around the world.

Seeds are often a great replacement for nuts. They bring some of the same texture and flavour, have many nutritional advantages, and are great for the environment. Here is my shortlist of nuts and seeds from my kitchen:

- Chia seeds
- Flax seeds
- Lotus seeds
- Peanuts
- Pumpkin seeds
- Sesame seeds
- Sunflower seeds
- Walnuts
- Occasionally choose brazil nuts, hazelnuts, pistachios, and cashews

BEANS AND LENTILS

I love beans and lentils, and you'll find every colour and flavour in my pantry, from India and Canada and all the places in between. I decant them into glass containers and line them up by variety and how they fit into my meals. Stored correctly, these environmental superheroes will last for years.

Read more about them in the "Pulses Are Perfect" section (page 42); meanwhile here is a short list to ease you into cooking more with legumes.

Any and all lentils, for example:
- Black lentils
- French lentils
- Green moong daal, also known as whole moong lentils
- Red lentils
- Yellow split moong daal or lentils

Any and all beans, for example:
- Adzuki beans
- All heritage beans
- Black and brown beans
- Chickpeas
- Dried peas like black-eyed or green
- Fava beans
- Red kidney beans—small and large
- White beans—navy, cannellini, lima, and more

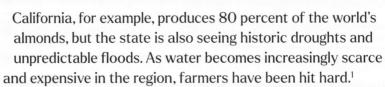

Most nuts are thirsty, resource-intensive crops, and when we grow them in areas that are limited in water and other resources the crops may need, we do irreparable harm to local natural ecosystems. Almonds in particular are nutritious and delicious, but as a crop, they need water, perhaps more than all the others, because of where and how they're grown.

California, for example, produces 80 percent of the world's almonds, but the state is also seeing historic droughts and unpredictable floods. As water becomes increasingly scarce and expensive in the region, farmers have been hit hard.[1]

CANNED, JARRED, AND PACKAGED ITEMS

As you may have noticed by now, I believe, wholeheartedly and deeply, that homemade, from-scratch food is greatly superior in flavour and nutrition; it is also a more planet-friendly way to eat. This is partly to do with how processed and resource intensive many foods are. Having said that, cooked and canned legumes and veggies are an excellent way to ease kitchen routines and check the Eating with Benefits strategies. They come with so much fast flavour and fibre! The convenience of opening a can of red kidney beans on a busy Wednesday night and repurposing leftovers from Sunday's roast chicken is just unbeatable.

Here's my short list of somewhat processed foods you will find in my pantry:

- Canned beans and lentils, all kinds
- Canned fish, sustainably sourced
- Canned vegetables in water or oil: chilies, baby corn, and corn kernels
- Cocoa powder
- Coconut milk and cream, creamed coconut, organic
- Condensed milk
- Dried fruits, including dates, apricots, raisins, cranberries, and figs
- Dried seaweed
- Evaporated milk
- Fish sauce
- Nut and seed butter, peanut butter, and tahini
- Nutritional yeast
- Orange marmalade, for marinades and sauces
- Tamarind pulp and paste
- Tomatoes—whole, crushed, passata, and sauce
- Vinegar—rice wine, apple cider, white, and balsamic

Avoid canned and jarred foods with a long list of ingredients. The labels should state what's inside: the food, some liquid (oil, water, brine, etc.) and possibly a way to preserve (a form of salt perhaps). That's it.

Avoid ultra-processed foods like sweet and salty snacks, canned soup, and breakfast cereals as much as possible. In general, these are known to be less healthy and more resource intensive. They also create way more waste in production and packaging than their less processed versions.[2]

OILS AND FATS

- Ghee
- Olive oil
- Occasionally sunflower and rice bran oil, coconut oil, sesame oil, and peanut oil

PANTRY VEGETABLES

- Garlic
- Ginger
- Jicama
- Onions, shallots
- Potatoes—white, yellow, purple, and sweet
- Pumpkins, whole (can be stored for many months)
- Winter squashes, hardy varieties can be stored for many weeks
- Yams

Note: Beets, carrots, tomatoes, and avocados also thrive for a few days in a cool, dark pantry. Afterwards, move these veggies to a colder environment like a fridge.

A note on potatoes: I have nothing against this widely available tuber. In fact, it checks my boxes for many reasons: potatoes can be stored for months at a time and they are also nutritious. I do think that this vegetable is overused in Western cooking; we eat so many versions of potato. You may even spot potato starch, a highly processed derivative in the most unexpected foods. So, I often skip potatoes for something else. Try sunchokes, sweet potatoes, or yams for a similar texture but deeper flavour.

Fridge and Freezer Staples

The refrigerator is a wondrous, glorious place. It can hold not only fruits and veggies but also parboiled grains, half-cooked meals, and leftovers that will bring dinner to the table on chaotic weeknights when we most need rescuing. The only obstacle is finding the leftovers before it's too late.

Here's a short list of fridge staples that I often keep around:

- Fruits, all sorts, including citruses like limes, lemons, and oranges
- Vegetables, switched out based on what is available, affordable, and in season:
  - Asparagus (in season for a brief time in early summer)
  - Beets with tops
  - Broccoli and broccoli rabe
  - Cauliflower
  - Cabbage
  - Carrots with tops
  - Chili peppers, all sizes, colours, and heat levels
  - Fenugreek leaves
  - Green beans
  - Green leaves, all sorts—spinach and kale, bok choy, watercress, etc.
  - Mushrooms
  - Peppers, all colours
- Fresh herbs, sometimes on my windowsill, other times in the fridge
- Almost always makrut lime leaves, lemon grass, and fresh curry leaves, which last for weeks
- Eggs
- Cheeses (the fermented and aged kinds have their own space in my fridge)
- Meats and fish make an appearance too

How to store cooked leftovers:
Use transparent containers and label them with a marker. And when you're ready to eat, remix them into something new and fun. Add a sauce, make a fritter, or make fried rice; there's no fun in eating the same meal twice.

FERMENTED FOODS

Eating a variety of fermented foods is good for our gut health and immunity, and our overall health too. In addition, fermentation adds great value because it helps to extend the life of veggies and in some cases even grains in the fridge. But the activity itself sounds boring, right? So, let's change that.

What if we thought of fermentation as a means of time travel? For generations, people and communities have used various techniques to preserve food to make it last from when it is widely available in times of abundance, mostly summer, to when our bodies need nourishment, i.e. winter. Take, for instance, the basket of fresh, locally sourced, organic, and brilliantly orange turmeric that I stumbled upon at the farmers' market last year at the end of what had been a fruitful season. While I initially bought the turmeric for the purpose of photography for this book, I'm now truly enjoying the bounty months later in the form of sun-fermented Turmeric Root Pickle (page 124).

Here are some fermented foods that you'll often see in my fridge, some made at home, the rest store bought:

- Buttermilk and yogurt (recipe on page 84)
- Cheese, various fermented varieties
- Indian pickles, turmeric pickle (page 124)
- Kanji, or sun-fermented pickles (page 135)
- Kefir
- Kimchi, or other varieties of pickled cabbage
- Kombucha
- Miso paste, organic
- Quick-pickled veggies (page 87)
- Tempeh

Freezer tips: The freezer is a great solution that buys us time and helps us actually eat the food we can't get to in time.

Too much fruit and veg? Freeze. What you lose in texture, you gain in longevity.

Bought two heads of broccoli? Eat one. Rinse, chop, and freeze the other.

What about nuts and flours? Store them in the pantry if you're using them within three months; otherwise, freeze them for longer life.

Too many leafy greens? Steam them, press the water out, and then freeze them.

Baguettes left over from the weekend? Freeze them, and then months later, on your busiest weeknight, when dinner seems hard, make No-Waste Golden Bread Upma (page 147).

Herbs and Spices

Dried herbs and spices are so important that they deserve their own section within this chapter.

Frankly, food tastes better with a little heat and spice, so it should come as no surprise to anyone here to learn that for generations armies were moved and kingdoms were won and lost in the pursuit of spices. Too soon for a colonization joke?

Spice is life, for many cultures around the world. Along with their aroma and flavour, spices are also used for their nutritional and medicinal properties. In Indian households, for example, you'll often see digestive aids like fennel seeds and ginger added to dishes with beans and meat to help with digestion. Tamarind and lime juice are rich in vitamin C, and I have learnt to add them for their sourness *and* their immunity-boosting qualities. A pinch of carom seeds, or *ajwain*, is often added to hot oil to heal just about everything gut related.

Delightfully though, you don't need an entire supermarket aisle of choices to create delicious flavour and aroma.

How to buy: Look for words like *heritage, original, sun-dried, single origin, fair-trade,* and/or *organic.* Some countries regulate their farms too. Shorter, more transparent supply chains improve the quality of the spice, its smell, and how the food tastes at the end of it all.

Did you know: Spices are similar to wine, coffee, and cocoa in that origin and blends matter. How and at what temperature the spices were roasted will influence the flavour, as will the direction of sun the plant was exposed to as it grew.

Black pepper used to be called black gold, and the world's best variety was originally from India. This spice is a berry that grows in beautiful green clusters that are harvested, briefly roasted, and then left out to dry. That's how we end up with the seed-like black pepper we are all familiar with.

Cardamom is often called the queen of spice because of its unique flavour and aroma. It is one of the three most expensive spices by weight, along with saffron and vanilla. The green husks are the seed pods found within the flower of the plant, and they can be picked only by hand. In addition to green, cardamom comes in a larger, lumpier, black variety too. I use the latter in many savoury dishes in this book.

Whole nutmeg is the seed inside the fruit. It is harvested from trees that take around 20 years to mature and flower.

The best cinnamon in the world comes from Sri Lanka. It is the bark of the tree that is first peeled away, soaked in water, dried, and then packed together in clusters. The most aromatic varieties come from farms that do all of this without harming the trees.

THE INTERNET'S TIMELESS DEBATE: WHOLE VS. GROUND

I am asked this question at cooking workshops and demonstrations all the time! Here's my view: both whole and ground spices have their place and time in building flavours while cooking.

Whole spices last a long time in jars, have deeper flavours and are flexible in how they can be used. For example, you can use them whole and also roast and grind them in a spice grinder to make your own customized blend. Add whole spices at the start of cooking along with the fat, as it takes time to draw out the flavours.

Ground spices are added halfway through the cooking process to retain the aroma as much as possible; some varieties go in right at the end, just as the dish is coming together.

The best dishes with flavours that sparkle are spiced in layers at various points in the cooking process, and use both whole and ground spices.

How to store: Store-bought, mass-produced, powdered spices tend to turn rancid quickly; blends, even faster. Buy in small batches if you can. Store whole spices in a glass container in a cool, dry area for a year or more. Powdered spices store for six months and blends for no more than three.

Cooking Hack:
No time to roast or grind whole spices? Shortcut your own spice blend using single-origin spice powders. Try various proportions of black pepper, cumin, coriander, and turmeric powders to make your own favourite dry rub.

Made My Mom's Garam Masala Blend (page 133)? Add a generous sprinkle right at the end on top of daal or stew as a treat for the senses.

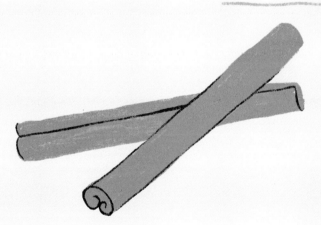

OUTFITTING THE MASALA DABBA (YOUR EVERYDAY SPICE BOX)

There's just something about opening the *masala dabba* that fires up my creativity and curiosity. The traditional version of this box usually contains five or seven little containers that hold the most commonly used spices. These are often switched out depending on the season and the family's preferences. Some spices like fennel and star anise are considered warming spices while coriander seeds are cooling in nature. In addition to what's in the box, people use many other spices during cooking. I use multiple combinations depending on my preference, the season, their flavour and aroma, and also their medicinal and nutritional properties.

In the masala dabba, I usually have:
- Cinnamon bark and powder
- Coriander seeds and powder
- Cumin seeds and powder
- Fennel seeds and powder
- Turmeric powder

In small jars or containers in my drawer, you will find:

WHOLE
- Black mustard seeds
- Black peppercorns
- Cardamom, green and black
- Carom seeds, or ajwain
- Fenugreek seeds
- Nutmeg, whole
- Saffron
- Star anise
- Yellow mustard seeds

POWDERED
Most whole spices also come in powdered form. Additionally:
- *Amchoor*, or dried mango powder—this is made by first sun-drying unripe (green) mangoes and then crushing them into a powdered form. Along with lime juice and tamarind, amchoor is a commonly used souring agent in regional cuisines in India. It is highly concentrated so a little goes a long way, use approx. a third of the lime juice you would normally. How to store: in a glass jar for a year.
- Chili powder—red chili powder, Kashmiri chili (least potent), paprika, and cayenne. Find a variety of chili peppers that work for your palate.
- Hing, or asafetida is a strong, pungent spice that is derived from the resin of a variety of the fennel. It often comes in a powder form and is used to add deep flavours when onions or garlic are not available (or used).
- *Kala Namak*, black rock salt, or black salt is black volcanic salt mostly harvested from lakes in the Indian-Himalayan mountains. It's more sulphuric in nature and therefore far stinkier than it's more mellow and widely known pink variety.

DRIED LEAVES AND HERBS
- *Anardana*, or dried pomegranate seeds
- Bay leaves
- Curry leaves
- Dried orange peels
- *Kasoori Methi* or fenugreek leaves

A Few Things I've Learned about Cooking Good Food

MENU PLANNING DOESN'T WORK

Stick with me for a minute here. First, an admission: having a series of dishes in mind helps when you're out grocery shopping. Sometimes, though, plans are built around what we "should" do, for example, shop better, eat healthy, etc. These plans work only when they offer flexibility for real life and what you end up buying can change depending on what's available, the prices, what you have at home already, the seasonality, and above all what you actually want to eat.

So, in the end having a rigid weekly meal plan can take up more time and may even cause more food waste.

So, here's what I do! I loosely plan for the type of meals—school lunches, family dinner, after-school snacks—and let my pantry and the grocery store do the rest. Many of the recipes in this book have been tweaked multiple times according to what is seasonal and fits my budget that week.

SPEND SUNDAY AFTERNOONS COOKING

This has been the one big change since my kids were younger. You see, when they were little, Sunday afternoons would fly by hanging out with friends or playdates, or at birthday parties. Now they are spent doing homework (for the kids) and cooking (for me). This helps me get a head start for the week.

I'll be honest, though, home cooking is a thankless task. Don't get me wrong; there are immeasurable benefits, to our own health and in helping ease the acts of eating and living! But prepping, washing, and trimming veggies and then cooking it all and refrigerating and organizing is a toil. So come Sunday afternoon I make it fun. Switch the lights to mellow, turn the radio on, mull a cuppa something warm, and then acknowledge the joy and ease that one afternoon of prep will bring my family the entire week.

Cook a big pot of beans, any kind will do. Store them in their cooking water, and then add to the dish when you're cooking.

Steam four servings of whole grains such as quinoa, rice, or pot barley. Use them in salads, bowls, lunch boxes and under curries.

Cook Indian-style tomato and veg sauce. Think of this as a technique rather than a recipe that uses whatever veg you have in your fridge along with passata tomato sauce, turmeric, fennel seeds, garlic, and ginger. Simmer it all together for 30 minutes. Store it in the fridge, and add it to pasta and curries to speed up cooking time.

Skillet-roast cruciferous veggies like broccoli, cauliflower, and Brussels sprouts (page 191). These refrigerate and reheat very well, can be used to complement other dishes, and can also be sliced in quesadillas and diced in rice bowls.

Boil a couple of large non-potato tubers like yams or sunchokes. Peel and refrigerate them. Use them as you would potatoes.

Start some lentil sprouts (page 86); they will be ready on the fourth day, likely Thursday, which for me is the busiest night of the week.

Lastly, set milk aside to ferment to make yogurt (page 84). A fresh bowl of yogurt, filled with all the probiotic possibilities, will ease the stresses of the week.

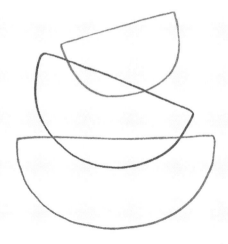

Choosing an induction stove for our kitchen was the best decision my husband and I made last year. These are more energy efficient, the temperature rises quickly with minimum waste, and there is less heat loss. Furthermore, the glass top remains cool enough to touch, so even if the cooking liquid boils over, there is no charring. For someone who hates cleaning the stove—that's me!—it's nice not to have burnt bits left behind.

While I see the value in stocking canned, jarred, and other shelf-stable items for a rainy day, I am not a fan of hoarding, mainly because it puts the people behind you in the checkout line at a disadvantage—there is less available for them. Also, funnily enough, in my experience as a mother, as soon as you buy an 8-pound bag of your kid's favourite food, your kids will have moved on!

#GOGREEN TIP: Baking a cake? Turning the oven on for just one dish or task is so 1990s. Multi-task your oven while the cake is baking for other activities such as roasting veggies, making granola, or even heating up dinner. You'll accomplish more in the same time, and use the same amount of energy.

Baking something small? Use a smaller appliance such as a toaster oven (with Energy Star rating). Larger appliances often take more time to heat and cook, and using them for smaller tasks is a waste of energy.

Buy what you and your family will eat and enjoy. All of this people- and planet-friendly advice works if there is enjoyment and the desire to repeat the behaviour day after day.

There's a misconception about green leafy vegetables: that they must be eaten raw and crisp to be healthy. And that's a big barrier for many of us because vegetables take the most time to prep. Getting the dirt off, rinsing, trimming the stems, peeling, etc. is a lot of work. Here's what I do: Once a week, I wash large bunches of everything green, cut away what isn't needed (set stems aside for Scrappy Stock, page 81), and then sauté them together with garlic and olive oil. Cook till the leaves have softened, and you're left with a mere fraction of the volume. This makes greens easier to store, and they last longer. Once cooked, they can also be tossed into any number of cooked stews, scrambled eggs, and curries, all week long. A wonderful way to eat more greens, and more frequently too!

Spend Sunday afternoons getting together with friends to cook big batches of vegetable sauce and chutney (page 112). Share it afterwards with your neighbours, your friends, and even strangers.

Whew! By no means is this an exhaustive list of everything you need to run a Good Food Kitchen. I hope this chapter, like everything else in this book, offers you a starting point in your journey toward cooking for your body and mind, as well as for the planet. This new way to cook and saving the planet may be uncomfortable and seem daunting in the beginning, and it will take patience. There may even be conflict within yourself and with others; just remind yourself that not all conflict is bad. After all, there is a long journey ahead of us, and we have to begin somewhere.

Chapter 4

Recipes with All the Benefits

You'll see the word *simple* numerous times in this section. I use it to describe many of the recipes here because often the ingredients are few, and each one serves a purpose in the dish, perhaps to add flavour or texture, or nutritional or medicinal benefits, or to boost gut health and immunity per the principles of Eating with Benefits. Still simple, I promise! Most of the ingredients included are accessible, within reach for most. Many of the recipes have been inspired by my roots in India and my family; others by my travels. Some dishes are good for rushed weeknight dinners, going from pantry/fridge to table in under 30 minutes, while others may be considered somewhat authentic and take longer with slower techniques. They have all been tested and tasted numerous times, by my friends and family and even by members of the *Maple and Marigold* community. Please enjoy.

How to Navigate the Recipes

Each recipe starts with important information about the dish: why the ingredient (or dish) made it into the book and how it checks my people- and planet-friendly boxes.

Regarding the number of servings, they are a loose guideline that needed some educated guesswork. After all, people's appetites and needs are different. Sometimes a bowl of daal along with some steam-cooked whole grains is a main in my home; other times the lentils will serve as a side dish to a larger meal.

The cooking times given in each recipe are based on months of testing and tasting. I often multi-task steps and cooking tasks though, and I suggest you do the same. For example, eggs can be boiled while the onions are caramelizing, chop ginger and garlic while the tomatoes are cooking, etc. The type of ingredients, the efficiency of the heat source, and even the number of times a pot is stirred during the cooking process can affect cook times. If you prefer to finish one step before moving on to the next, that's okay too! Do what works for you in your kitchen.

The main part of these recipes is the "Gather" (what you need) section followed by the "Make" section, where you will find the instructions. Most of the kitchen tools, foods, and ingredients that you will need are listed in chapter 3, "How to Stock a Good Food Kitchen." In general, that is a heavy-bottomed pot (8 or 10 inches in diameter) with a lid, a stainless-steel skillet or two (8 or 10 inches in diameter), and various tools such as knives, spatulas, and spoons. Make do with what you have as much as possible. If pan-frying, choose smaller pans; you'll use less cooking fat. For even cooking, avoid overcrowding.

For items other than those listed above, you will see an equipment note in the recipe.

LITTLE NUGGETS

This is the fun stuff, what I have learned over the years about making this new way of cooking easy or gut healthy and climate smart: you'll see them listed as Recipe Notes, How to Eat, Variations, Cooking Hacks, and, my favourite, #GoGreen Tips.

Cooking at home is boring and repetitive on a good day, and these little nuggets make it less so. In addition, they help ensure that you get the best results and help you adapt the dishes to what works for you.

RECIPE LEGEND

- *V* = Vegetarian
- *Vg* = Vegan
- *PF* = Pantry-forward, using mostly pantry ingredients
- *FF* = Freezer-friendly, can be frozen and reheated
- *HM* = Halve your meat recipe
- *LW* = Low-waste ingredients or tweaks

Note: You'll notice that most of the recipes are naturally gluten-free. I often swap all-purpose flour for chickpea flour. Most recipes are also dairy-free. Skip the ghee and many vegetarian dishes can also be made vegan.

Cornerstone Staples

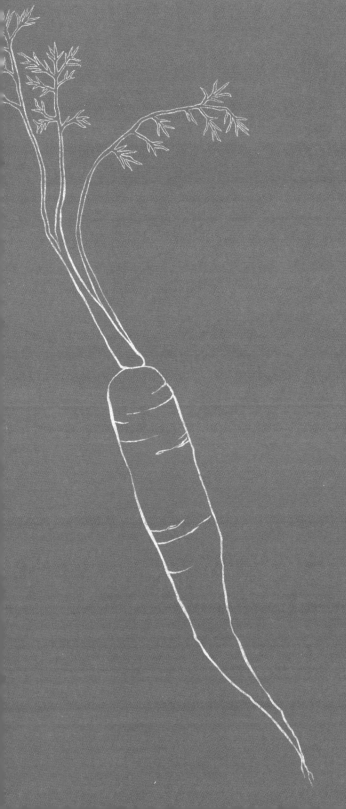

Scrappy Stock

V / *FF* / *LW*
2 hours
Makes 6 cups

GATHER

3 cups vegetable trimmings,
  for example:
- Asparagus ends
- Carrot peels and base
- Celery, fennel, and leek ends
- Cucumber and apple skins
- Ginger and garlic peels and bits
- Green bean and snap pea tails
- Onion ends (limit to ½ cup due
  to strong flavour)
- Potato peels

2 black cardamom pods
1 bay leaf
1 tsp fennel seeds
½ tsp peppercorns

There's a reason this recipe is first in this section. A good-quality stock can be a key building block for infinite meals. Coincidentally, this recipe is also easy to follow, mostly hands-free, and helps reduce waste in the kitchen. To make this stock, I collect vegetable scraps and peels and ends of this and that in a jar in the fridge all week long, and then come Sunday afternoon everything goes into a big pot to simmer for an hour or two. That's it—joy with ease; it's the best kind.

MAKE

Rinse the vegetable trimmings and place them in a big soup pot. Add enough water to cover everything. *Note:* Some of the water will evaporate during the cooking process, so start with as much as your pot will hold and add more as needed.

Bring it to a boil and then reduce the heat to a simmer. Add the whole spices and continue to simmer for 1½ hours. Turn the heat off.

After the liquid has cooled, strain the mixture out. Press out every last drop of stock from the bits in the strainer to draw out the flavour and nutritional goodness.

Use the stock straightaway or refrigerate it for up to a week. You can also freeze it in freezer-friendly glass jars for up to 5 months. Thaw and use as needed.

HOW TO EAT
Use in risotto, daal, stew, pulao, biryani, soup, etc.

VARIATIONS
Corn stock: Reserve rinsed corn husks and cobs (use organic if available). Skip the other trimmings and aromatics to allow the flavour of the corn to shine. Use in No-Waste Corn and Barley-sotto (page 193).

Chicken stock: Put the leftover carcass of a whole roast chicken in the soup pot, including the bones, cartilage, etc., along with the vegetable trimmings. Simmer for 2 hours, turn the heat off, and follow the remaining steps.

No Fruit Left Behind Compote

Vg / FF / LW
30 minutes
Makes 4 cups

GATHER

4 cups overripe fresh fruit, any kind
    (see variations)
4 Tbsp cane sugar (or brown sugar or
    maple syrup) (approx.)
2 tsp lime juice (approx. ½ lime)
Water as needed, starting with ½ cup

I don't remember ever seeing fruit being thrown away when I was growing up. Before heading to the farmers' market—or the veggie *thela* cart that would pull up outside our house—my mom would check the fridge and take a quick inventory so she knew what was still in there. If there was too much fruit one week, or if unexpected bruises emerged, my mom would wash the fruit and then dump it all in a pan and make a sauce. Several years ago, I discovered that the fruit sauce my mom made every week to avoid food waste was a variation of French compote—a rather straightforward method that extracts flavour and beauty from a bowl of mushy, past-its-best fruit.

MAKE

Rinse the fruit and trim any mouldy bits. Add the fruit, sugar, lime juice and water to a saucepan and turn the heat to medium. Bring the mixture to a boil and then turn it down to simmer for about 30 minutes. Add more water if the mixture looks like it's drying up. I cook the fruit down until it is soft and has just lost its shape. Cook time will vary depending on the fruit.

Taste for sweetness and add more sugar if needed. Chill and refrigerate in a clean jar with a lid for up to 2 weeks.

This sauce can also be frozen and then thawed and used as needed.

VARIATIONS
I love this sauce plain, but sometimes spices add a touch of elegance. Here are some fruit and spice combinations that work:

*   Peaches, nectarines + nutmeg
*   Skin-on apples + cinnamon
*   Blueberries, strawberries + vanilla
*   Skin-on grapes (green, pink or red), no spices needed

RECIPE NOTE
If a lot of liquid has been released by the fruit and the consistency is runny, you can add ½ tsp chia seeds and chill the mixture for 30 minutes. Chia seeds are hydrophilic and will absorb the extra liquid.

HOW TO EAT
Drizzle on yogurt for breakfast or use as a topping for dessert.

How to Make Yogurt at Home

V / LW
25 minutes +
overnight fermentation
Makes 4 cups

GATHER

4 cups whole (or 2%) milk (long-life
milk that comes in Tetra Paks does
not ferment well)
1 Tbsp starter with live cultures

Equipment
Glass container large enough to hold
the yogurt (ceramic and clay work too),
or several small containers; kitchen
thermometer (optional)

In India, yogurt, or *dahi*, as I grew up calling it, is served with
every main meal. The reason for this accompaniment goes far
deeper than it being simply a means to cool off the palate after
a bite of spicy food. For generations, grandmothers have been
fermenting milk to make yogurt, week after week, adding it to
everyday meals as a way to soothe and nourish their families.
Today, I am thrilled to pass this wisdom about fermentation and
accessible food on to you and yours—bowl after bowl of probiotic goodness that can be made at home with just two ingredients: milk and starter. (Recipe pictured on page 82.)

MAKE

Rinse a saucepan and pour the milk in. Turn the heat to medium-
high and bring the milk to a boil. This takes about 5–7 minutes. Stay
vigilant because once bubbles form on the surface of the milk, the
milk will rise quickly and may bubble over. Turn the heat off and
let the milk cool to a warm temperature, about 10 minutes. Use the
"pinky test" to confirm. The temperature is right when you can dip
your pinky finger into the milk comfortably without it feeling too
hot or too cold. It should feel just warm. That's the perfect temperature to begin the transformation of milk into yogurt. (For those
who like exact measurements, pinky-ready milk is 110°F/43°C.)

While you wait for the milk to be pinky ready, take the starter out
of the fridge. Use the back of a spoon to smear 1 Tbsp of starter on
the bottom of the glass container. If using multiple containers, you
will need the same ratio of starter to milk and the same technique.

Pour the cooled milk into the glass container, submerging the starter.
Stir gently 8–10 times with the back of the spoon, forming 8s if possible in the bowl. Cover with a napkin or plate. Do not close tightly.

Place the covered glass container in a warm corner of the kitchen
for 6–8 hours. I usually leave the bowl overnight in a cold oven with
the oven light on. (**Note:** Milk changes to yogurt due to the formation of bacteria. For bacteria to form, there needs to be warmth and
rest so that science can work its magic through the entire bowl of
milk. Too-hot milk may cause spoilage. Too cool may discourage the
formation of enough bacteria. During the warm summer months,
yogurt can be set in as little as 4 hours.)

Once the milk has fermented into yogurt, place the container in the fridge for 2 hours, up to a week. Chilled yogurt has a thicker consistency. Use as needed. Reserve 1 Tbsp as starter to make yogurt the following week.

HOW TO EAT

Eat plain yogurt with sugar or dried fruit if you like it sweet, or with salt and cumin seeds as a side. You can also use homemade yogurt in marinades and dressings, or whisk it with chopped cucumbers and mint leaves to make a raita.

VARIATIONS

Prefer thicker, almost Greek-style yogurt? Strain chilled yogurt in a cheesecloth or mesh strainer in the fridge for a day or two. One day of straining will yield Greek-style yogurt. Two days of straining and you will end up with labneh, which has an almost cream cheese–like texture.

#GOGREEN TIP
If the newly fermented yogurt hasn't set all the way, don't throw it away. Use the milk to make paneer (page 95). And try for yogurt another day.

What is starter?

It's a sample culture of bacteria used to ferment milk into yogurt. It can be 1 Tbsp from a previous batch of yogurt or a store-bought starter culture (some health food stores carry it), or one can ferment milk by using naturally occurring bacteria found in the environment. If you are using store-bought yogurt for starter, check the label for words like *organic*, *active culture*, and *lactobacillus*. There should be very few other ingredients.

Starter failed?

Use a whole green chili to help the fermentation process along! Add it—with the stalk on—into the milk before covering the glass container. The naturally occurring bacteria in the stem of a fresh green chili are similar to the bacteria required to make yogurt. There may be a mild but distinct flavour to the yogurt so use this batch to make a vanilla and fruit smoothie and save 1 Tbsp for the starter for the next batch of yogurt. The aftertaste disappears after a cycle or two of fermentation.

You can also try swapping out the starter for another brand of yogurt. I went through several iterations before I found a local, small-batch-dairy yogurt that worked well.

How to Sprout Whole Lentils

Vg / PF / LW
3 days or more
Makes 4 cups

GATHER

1 cup whole, skin-on lentils (start with
   the green moong bean variety)

Equipment
Large, deep bowl; cotton dish towel
or square of cheesecloth

COOKING HACK

For faster germination, use a small cotton sack made with light-weight fabric instead of a dishtowel. On Day 2 transfer soaked lentils into it, sprinkle water periodically, shake to air, and continue method as usual.

HOW TO EAT

Rinse with cold water before eating. Toss with cilantro, lime juice, and diced tomatoes and enjoy on Indian-Style Bruschetta (page 151). Longer sprouts can be tossed with noodles, rice, or stir-fries.

#GOGREEN TIP
Tiny moong beans are prized by people in South and Southeast Asia for their crisp taste and nutritional richness. Farmers love them too. They come highly recommended in the Future 50 Foods report published by the World Wildlife Fund and Knorr (see Notes and Recommended Reading, pages 258–260).

Sprouting triples the nutritional benefits of dried lentils. That's saying a lot when you consider that lentils and beans are already referred to as some of the most people- and planet-friendly foods. I get that sprouting can seem complicated, though; there are multiple steps and tools, and rest time in between stages. In this recipe, I show how sprouting can offer everyone, even during times of restrictions, access to easy, kitchen-grown, delicious, and nourishing *fresh* food.

MAKE

Day 1: Rinse the lentils in cool water a couple of times and place them in a large, deep bowl. Add enough water to cover with a couple of inches to spare. Soak overnight, about 6–8 hours.

Day 2: In the morning, discard the water and rinse the lentils again. Leave them damp and cover them with a damp dish towel or square of cheesecloth. Set the bowl of lentils aside in a quiet corner of the kitchen. Set the oven timer for 8 hours.

In the evening, remove the cloth and toss the lentils with your fingers to allow air to circulate around the grains. (*Note:* sprouts require moisture and good air circulation to form and flourish.) By now the seeds should be starting to germinate. Replace the cloth, sprinkle a few tablespoons of water on the fabric, and leave the bowl overnight. Set the oven timer to check in 8 hours.

Day 3: Repeat the air-and-sprinkle-water technique. This allows the lentils to continue to sprout. By now the seed sprouts should be germinated enough to be eaten. At this stage, you could move the bowl to the fridge, where the sprouting will stop but the sprouts will keep for up to 5 days. Keep the dish towel damp while in the refrigerator.

Want longer sprouts? Repeat the day 3 steps for another day or two to allow the sprouts to grow out. Around day 6, you may see tiny leaves on the white stems. These microgreens are edible and delicious.

How to Quick-Pickle Hard Veggies

Vg / LW
20 minutes
Makes 2 cups

GATHER

1 cup rice wine (or distilled white) vinegar

1 cup water

2 Tbsp sugar

½ tsp salt

2 cups crunchy vegetables, cut into 1-inch batons or sliced, for example:

- Beets
- Cabbage
- Carrots
- Cucumbers
- Hot peppers
- Radishes
- Red onions
- Turnips

Equipment

Glass jar, with lid, large enough to fit the veggies and liquid mixture, or several smaller jars

I believe pickling is a life skill. And as someone who craves the salty, sour, crunchy texture of pickled chilies and veggies, speedy pickling is a dream. This method is different from that used for Sun-Fermented Kanji (page 135); this doesn't develop as deep, funky flavours. It is also very different from the more time-intensive achar pickles of India; quick-pickling doesn't have the probiotic richness that comes with longer fermentation times. However, this technique helps in-season produce last longer, adds an unmistakable sparkle to bean- and veggie-forward dishes, and reminds us that good food, the best food, doesn't need much to make it shine.

MAKE

In a heavy-bottomed saucepan, bring the vinegar and water to a boil. Turn the heat off. Add the sugar and salt and stir to dissolve. Pack the vegetables into the glass jar, pour the hot liquid on top, and let it stand to cool.

Once it's cool, put the lid on the jar and store it in the refrigerator for up to 3 weeks. The crunchiness will start to mellow out by day 3.

HOW TO EAT

Enjoy immediately once cooled, but the flavours really pop after a day in the fridge. The pickles can be added to lentils and bean dishes, with chapatti on the side. One of my favourite ways to eat them is tucked into the Calcutta-Style Kathi Rolls (page 227).

Make-It-Your-Own Veggie and Lentil Fritters

Vg / PF / FF
35 minutes
Makes 8 fritters

GATHER

1 cup split red lentils (masoor daal)
1 cup water
½ + ⅓ tsp salt (approx.)
⅓ + ½ tsp turmeric powder
1 cup cauliflower florets
1 cup finely diced mild red onions
¼ cup chickpea flour
2 Tbsp chia seeds
1 Tbsp finely chopped garlic
1 Tbsp sesame seeds
2 Tbsp grape-seed oil
Chopped cilantro to taste

Equipment
Microwaveable bowl; microwave

Fritters are my absolute favourite way to eat veggies and lentils together. This recipe is inspired by the traditional deep-fried *shami kebabs* and is an absolute gem of a dish. I have tweaked the steps to be easier to follow; it's more or less a formula that you can use to cook with what you have, and what you and your family feel like that week. Swap out the red lentils for yellow, and the cauliflower for carrots, zucchini, or even broccoli.

MAKE

Rinse the lentils a couple of times in a saucepan and drain. Add the water, ½ tsp of the salt, and ⅓ tsp of the turmeric. Bring to a boil, then simmer, covered, for 12–15 minutes on medium-low heat.

Check that the lentils are done by squishing a few grains with a spoon. They should mash, but not too easily. Turn off the heat and leave the lentils covered.

While the lentils are cooking, place the cauliflower in the bowl with enough water to cover the florets. Microwave, covered, on high heat until half cooked, 2 minutes. Let cool.

Finely chop the cauliflower and add it to the cooked lentils in the saucepan. Add the onions, chickpea flour, chia seeds, garlic, sesame seeds, the remaining ½ tsp turmeric, and ⅓ tsp salt (if needed), and mash together with the lentils and cauliflower until everything is well mixed. Set aside for 10 minutes to allow time for the chia seeds to do their hydrophilic magic.

While the mixture is resting, place a skillet on the stove on medium heat. Drizzle 1 Tbsp of the oil into the pan and allow it to heat through.

Scoop 1 Tbsp of batter at a time into the oil; 4–5 fritters should fit in the pan at a time. Press down to flatten them slightly. Cook the fritters until they look light brown and crispy, 4–5 minutes on the first side, and 2–3 minutes on the other. Remove them to a plate while you cook the remaining batter in the remaining 1 Tbsp of oil. Garnish with the cilantro.

COOKING HACK

Triple the recipe and freeze the extra fritters. Pan-fry them partially, 2 minutes on each side, cool and freeze. Thaw and pan-fry for a couple of minutes to make them crispy once again!

#GOGREEN TIP

Cooked lentils left over from last week? Use them to make these fritters. Leftover veggies? Cook them further to mash and add to the lentils instead of cauliflower.

RECIPE NOTE

Depending on the humidity that day, the age of the lentils, and the moisture released by the vegetables, the consistency of the batter can vary. If the batter seems too runny, use an extra teaspoon of chia seeds to absorb the excess moisture.

HOW TO EAT

Serve with a crisp salad, or, as is common in India, between 2 slices of bread with pickled veggies and a dollop of yogurt on the side.

Basic Way to Cook Beans

Vg | PF | FF
Overnight soaking +
2 hours cooking
Makes 4 cups

GATHER

1 cup dried chickpeas
½ tsp fennel seeds
¼ tsp salt
5 cups water (approx.)

Equipment
Large bowl; Instant Pot (optional)

There's always back and forth on the topic of how to cook beans. A quick internet search will offer a whole lot of confusion. To soak or not? Use dried beans or not? There are many debates over how to cook beans from scratch. My favourite method is also, in my opinion, the easiest way to cook beans. Incredibly enough, one can start with a pot of dry, boring, dormant seeds and transform them into a mellow, nourishing, and people- and planet-friendly dish.

MAKE

Rinse the beans and soak them overnight in a large bowl with enough water to cover the beans with a couple of inches to spare.

Discard the soaking water, rinse the beans, and place them in a large pot. Add the fennel seeds and salt, and cover with 5 cups water. Turn the heat to high, bring to a boil, and then turn the heat down to a medium simmer. Cover the pot with a lid.

Check on the beans every 10 minutes. Add more water if needed. The beans are done when they're tender, about 2 hours. Cooking time may vary depending on the type of chickpea and how old the beans are.

Using an Instant Pot? Place the chickpeas in the inner pot, add the fennel seeds and salt, and cover with water. Cook on high pressure for 18 minutes. Do a natural pressure release for 5 minutes.

Store the chickpeas and the nutrition-rich cooking water for up to a week in the fridge, and for up to 6 months in the freezer.

COOKING HACKS

Adding fennel seeds or ginger when cooking lentils can help ease digestion and the feeling of bloating that some people experience after eating them.

Forgot to soak the chickpeas overnight? Use hot water and soak for an hour instead. Extend the cooking time until the beans are squishy when squeezed.

VARIATIONS

You can cook any whole bean using this method. The soaking and cooking times will vary, but chickpeas take the longest compared with others, so plan accordingly.

Basic Way to Cook Whole Lentils

Vg / PF
30 minutes soaking +
40 minutes cooking
Makes 3 cups

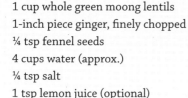

GATHER

1 cup whole green moong lentils
1-inch piece ginger, finely chopped
¼ tsp fennel seeds
4 cups water (approx.)
¼ tsp salt
1 tsp lemon juice (optional)

Equipment
Large bowl; Instant Pot (optional)

Whole lentils are the quiet heroes of the legume world and come in many shades of black, brown, and green. They are considered whole because they have not been split or husked and retain more of the outer layers of the seed. As a result, they are firmer in texture, are more nutritious, and have a robust and nutty flavour. Much like beans, whole lentils can take a while to cook. Thankfully, also like beans, they are quite hands-off.

MAKE

Rinse the lentils and soak them in warm water for 30 minutes. Discard the water, rinse again, and place the lentils in a pot. Add the ginger and fennel seeds and cover with 4 cups water. Turn the heat to high and bring to a boil. Now turn the heat down to a medium simmer, cover the pot with a lid, and cook until the lentils are tender, 40 minutes. You may need to add more water during the cooking process to keep the lentils submerged. Once the lentils are cooked, season them with the salt and lemon juice (if using).

Using an Instant Pot? Pour soaked lentils and other ingredients in and cook on high for 10 minutes. Natural release.

Store in the fridge for up to 5 days, or freeze for up to 6 months.

HOW TO EAT

Use in curries and stews to add protein, flavour, and texture. Swap out meat for any variety of whole lentils, or serve on the side with a hot oil and spice tadka.

VARIATIONS

Split lentils take less time to cook. Try with all sorts of lentils and experiment with cooking times and seasonings.

How to Make Paneer

V / LW
40 minutes
Makes 4 servings

GATHER

5 cups whole milk
1½ tsp lime juice (approx.)

Equipment
Strainer or cheesecloth; comfortably
sized mixing bowl

Paneer is a fresh, soft, non-melting cheese that is widely eaten across the Indian subcontinent. It is one of my favourite foods to make from scratch because you need only two ingredients, milk and lime juice, to transform everyday, routine milk into something extraordinary. Fresh cheese! Even more, you don't need a whole lot of tools, space, or expertise to follow these steps.

MAKE

Pour the milk into a heavy-bottomed saucepan and bring it to a gentle boil. Stir gently and keep the lime juice handy. Be prepared to move quickly once the bubbles form.

Once you see rolling bubbles cover the surface of the milk, turn the stove off to stop the milk from boiling over. Now turn it back on at the lowest heat setting possible. Add the lime juice directly into the milk. Stir gently and you'll see the milk solids and whey start to separate. If the separation is slow to appear, add another few drops of lime juice to the milk. Lime juice is acidic and helps to separate the milk solids from the whey, but you may need a little more than expected depending on how the milk was processed where you live.

Turn the stove off and allow the separation process to complete. Stir gently and allow the whey to clear and cool. At room temperature, the whey should turn a very pale green colour.

Place a strainer over a mixing bowl and pour the curds and whey mixture through to collect the solid curds. You just made paneer.

Note: If the curds smell lemony, pour ½ cup cold water through the strainer to rinse them. Let the curds stand in the strainer to allow the excess liquid to drain away. This takes about 20 minutes.

I often stop at this stage; mellow, smooth paneer is great to eat as is.

HOW TO EAT
Homemade paneer curds are delicious with chopped cilantro and black pepper on toast, or with a drizzle of honey. Cook paneer curds with cumin seeds, onions, garlic, and ginger to make a paneer scramble.

Cornerstone Staples 95

Shape the paneer curds by transferring them onto a cheesecloth. Knot the cloth around the curds and place on a plate. Rest a heavy weight such as a cast iron pan on top of the knotted bundle and let the paneer rest for 2 hours. You will be left with a flattened tablet that resembles what you get in a grocery store. This block can be refrigerated for up to 3 days. Slice into cubes and cook as needed. Use for Any Greens Saag Paneer (page 187).

> #GOGREEN TIP
> Milk a couple of days past its best-before date? Make paneer (see food waste links in Notes and Recommended Reading, pages 258–260).
>
> Whey to go! Use the leftover whey as a nutritious, tangy and flavourful addition to smoothies, chapatti dough, pancakes and muffins, and also to stews and soups.

How to Cook Any Whole Grain

Vg / PF / FF
30 minutes soaking +
45 minutes cooking
Makes 6 servings

GATHER

1 cup hulled barley (light brown
   in colour)
3 cups water
1 tsp ghee
¼ tsp salt

Beautiful, healthy whole grains! They're good for our gut and great for the planet, but as it turns out we don't eat as much of this delicious food as we should. That's because people find cooking whole grains complicated and time consuming. I did too until a few years ago; *so many steps*, I thought. Here's my one big tip: whole grains cook faster when they're soaked for half an hour in warm water. This makes them easier to digest too. Short on time? Whole grains like millet or pseudocereals like amaranth, quinoa, and buckwheat have all the advantages of whole grains but can be cooked in as little as 20 minutes.

MAKE

Rinse the grains 3–4 times in cool water. Soak in warm water for 30 minutes.

Drain and place the barley in a saucepan. Add 3 cups water along with the ghee and salt. Bring it to a boil, then turn it down to a low simmer. Cover with a lid and cook for 40 minutes.

Test for doneness: The barley is cooked when steam tunnels form and most of the water has been absorbed into the grains. Bite into a couple of grains to confirm that they are cooked through. Hulled barley is chewy and nutty in flavour. Turn the heat off and leave the lid on for 5 minutes.

Once the grains are cooked, remove the pot from the heat and fluff them with a fork. Let them sit for a few minutes before serving.

VARIATIONS

Follow these same steps for tougher whole grains like whole oats, farro, wheat, spelt, millet, and brown rice. For grains like freekeh, buckwheat, amaranth, bulgur, and quinoa, skip the soaking time and cook using a ratio of 1 part grains to 2.5 parts water, for 20–25 minutes.

HOW TO EAT

Serve with a dollop of ghee alongside any of the dishes in this book. Toss with sprouted lentils, chopped cucumber and tomatoes and a Tbsp lime juice to make an incredible salad!

Freezer tip: Cook a double batch of whole grains and freeze half for up to 6 months. Thaw for a day in the fridge, add a Tbsp or two of water and microwave on high, covered for 4 minutes, use as needed.

2-Ingredient Whole Grain Flatbread (Chapatti)

V / PF / FF
30 minutes + resting time
Makes 8 chapattis

GATHER

1 cup atta flour
1 cup water (approx.)
Ghee, carom seeds, salt (optional)

Equipment

Paraat or high-sided plate (see picture); large bowl; rolling pin; large tawa or stainless steel frying pan; flat-edged tongs; a light-weight cotton tea towel

Chapatti, or roti, as it is also commonly called, is a traditional form of flatbread that is ubiquitous in Indian cuisine. It is often made with whole grain, whole wheat flour and is grilled just as everybody is gathering to sit down to eat. The best chapattis are fluffy and freshly made with just two ingredients, flour and water, which are kneaded together, shaped, rolled out, and cooked. That's it. No yeast, no oven, just your hands, a rolling pin, and the stove. Simple food for the soul that I finally became comfortable cooking during those early days of the pandemic.

MAKE

Add the flour to the paraat and start adding the water, a splash at a time. Knead. Add more water a little at a time and allow it to absorb into the flour. Kneading and folding will help the dough come together. This process takes about 8–9 minutes. As you knead, you'll notice the dough becoming more flexible and the bits and sprinkles from the corners of the paraat will come together. If cracks appear in the dough, it's too dry. Add a splash of water and then knead for another minute.

Shape the dough into a large ball, sprinkle a few drops of water, and cover it with a large bowl placed upside down over the dough. Let it rest for 45 minutes.

Uncover the dough and gently knead and fold it again. You should now be able to feel the elasticity and flexibility in the dough. This texture makes the chapattis soft and fluffy.

Divide the dough into 2½–3-inch peda, or balls. Loosely shape the balls of dough between the palms of your hands into rustic discs. Place each disc on a flat surface, such as a clean kitchen counter, and sprinkle a generous pinch of flour on it. Roll it out with the rolling pin. Add another sprinkle of flour, flip it, and roll it again. At this time you can smear a drop of ghee with the back of a spoon and sprinkle a pinch of carom seeds and salt on the dough. Roll it again. The dough will start to flatten out and move around, and you should end up with a thin, circular chapatti about 6–7 inches in diameter.

Place the tawa on the stove on high heat. Once the tawa is hot, lower the heat to medium and wipe the surface with a clean cloth. Place the chapatti on the tawa and allow it to cook until you see bubbles form in the dough, about 1 minute. Flip the chapatti, using tongs if needed. You should start to see parts of the chapatti puff up now! Gentle patting with a folded tea towel will help the chapatti puff some more. Cook on this side for 30 seconds and then remove from the pan. Serve hot with a smear of ghee or butter.

To store, cool chapattis completely and refrigerate for 3 days. You can also freeze chapattis in an airtight container. To reheat, thaw, add a sprinkle of water, cover and microwave on high in stacks of 2–3 for 30 seconds.

Morning Starts

Magic Not Mundane Chia Seed Pudding

Vg | PF
10 minutes + 2 hours
to soak overnight
Makes 4 servings

GATHER

14 oz (400 mL) can organic coconut milk
2 Tbsp chia seeds
3 tsp cane sugar or maple syrup
2–3 drops vanilla essence

Equipment
Comfortably sized container with lid

At first glance chia seeds look pretty ordinary, so you wouldn't know these tiny, black, oval seeds are a nutritional powerhouse. History traces these seeds back to the ancient Aztecs, who, legend has it, considered them important nourishment for their most powerful warriors.[1] Chia grows well in dry climates with low-quality soil and little human support, making them good for us and good for the planet, but the power of this ordinary-looking seed doesn't stop here. Chia seeds come naturally coated in a hydrophilic substance that, when left to rest in a liquid, absorbs the surrounding liquid and becomes almost gel-like. Magical, right? But then that's nature for you: even the ordinary has magic hiding underneath. (Recipe pictured on page 82.)

MAKE

Pour the coconut milk into the container. If the coconut water and cream have separated, whisk them together. Stir in the chia seeds, sugar, and vanilla essence. Cover and refrigerate for at least 2 hours, ideally overnight.

Remove from the fridge, stir, and enjoy.

HOW TO EAT
Top with coconut flakes, sliced mango or other fresh fruit, or As You Like It Granola (page 105) with No Fruit Left Behind Compote (page 83).

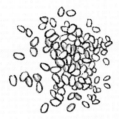

Use chia seeds as a binder instead of bread crumbs and eggs. These magical seeds not only bring mixtures together, they also absorb liquid and add protein and other nutritional benefits.[1]

As You Like It Granola

Vg / PF
25 minutes
Makes 4 servings

GATHER

⅓ cup peanut butter

¼ cup maple syrup (or honey)

2 cups oats (mix of rolled and instant)

¼ cup chopped nuts (mix of pecans and walnuts)

1 Tbsp brown sugar

1 Tbsp olive oil

1 tsp vanilla

½ cup chopped dried fruit

¼ cup seeds of your choice (sunflower or pumpkin work well)

Pinch of salt

Equipment

Mixing bowls; microwave; half-sheet baking pan; silicone mat

Morning cereal is a ritual in many families, as it used to be in ours. Unfortunately, it often includes highly processed, store-bought, plastic-intensive choices. This homemade, from-scratch granola is a medley of flavour and texture that represents the best of people- and planet-friendly food. It brings together the crunchy, chewy, and sweet that I adore. And it's made with pantry-forward, simple ingredients that we can tweak based on what we want to eat that week. Granola any way you like it!

MAKE

Preheat the oven to 330°F. Add the peanut butter and maple syrup to a microwaveable mixing bowl and heat on high for 30 seconds. Stir and microwave again until the mixture is mushy and syrupy, another 30 seconds.

In a large mixing bowl, toss the oats, nuts, sugar, olive oil, and vanilla with the peanut butter mixture. Place the silicone mat in the baking pan. Spread the granola mixture out in the pan and bake for a total of 20 minutes. At the 19-minute mark, take the pan out and add the dried fruit, seeds (if using), and a big pinch of salt. Toss, and put the pan back in the oven for another minute.

Remove the granola from the oven and let it cool completely. Snap off clusters and store in a glass container on the kitchen counter for up to 1 month.

HOW TO EAT

Serve with homemade yogurt (page 84) and fruit compote (page 83) for a well-balanced breakfast or snack.

Chewy, Crunchy Granola Crumble Bars

Vg | PF
40 minutes
Makes 16 bars

GATHER

For the Crumble

2 cups rolled oats
1½ cups plain quick oats
1 cup loosely packed brown sugar
¾ cup butter, softened
1 tsp baking powder
1 tsp vanilla essence

For the Filling

2 cups dried dates
½ cup hazelnuts, roasted and peeled
4 tsp cocoa

Equipment

Food processor, 8 × 8-inch baking pan

Dried fruits are magic. Think about it! Summer-fresh, plump fruits reduced to dried-up, wrinkled, intensely sweet nuggets. The appearance of the fruit changes but the flavour deepens, as do the nutritional benefits. And that's not even the best part. Let's consider dates for a minute. Fresh dates are available in a very small area of the world. But the dried varieties? Those can be found in almost every corner of the world. Magic you can taste when you bite into these bars.

MAKE

For the Crumble

Mix together all the ingredients with a hand blender or pastry cutter until well combined. Set aside.

For the Filling

Preheat the oven to 350°F.

Rehydrate the dates (see sidebar) and reserve the soaking water. Pit and chop the softened dates. In a food processor, blend the dates, hazelnuts, and cocoa until the mixture is smooth, about 5 minutes. Add some of the soaking water from the rehydrated dates if needed. When fully blended, the filling should be a thick, almost doughy consistency.

Grease the baking pan and start layering. Use half the oat crumble as the first layer on the bottom. The date filling goes on top of this layer; use the back of a spoon to press it down evenly. Add the remaining oat crumble and smooth it with the back of the spoon. Bake until the edges of the crumble brown, 25 minutes. Remove the pan from the oven and cool before slicing the crumble into bars.

Store in an airtight container on the counter for up to 1 week.

How to rehydrate dates:

Pour boiling hot water on the dried fruits. Use 2 cups of water for every cup of dates. Set the bowl aside for 30 minutes to soften the fruit. Use the soaking water in stews and for baking. This method can be used to rehydrate any dried fruit.

Savoury, Veggie-Forward Amaranth Porridge Upma

V | PF
30 minutes
Makes 4 servings

GATHER

1 cup amaranth seeds

1 Tbsp ghee

2 Tbsp peanuts, blanched and lightly chopped

1 Tbsp cashew nuts

1 tsp mustard seeds

2 dried whole red chilies

1 tsp finely chopped ginger

1 small finely chopped green chili (deseed if needed)

½ cup finely chopped onions

6–7 curry leaves (dried or fresh)

½ cup green peas (frozen or fresh)

2½ cups water

Salt to taste

1 tsp lime juice

Would it surprise you to learn that amaranth is an ancient seed that has been an important food and also a cultural symbol for more than 8,000 years? In northern India, amaranth is called *ramdana*, which translates to "grain of gods." Versatile, nutritious, easy to cook, and easy to grow, the grain of gods seems appropriately named.

Upma is a veggie-forward, nutty, savoury, totally delicious breakfast dish in India that's normally made with semolina flour. Here I make this recipe with amaranth, which goes beautifully with curry leaves and the spices that together make this ancient grain shine.

MAKE

In a medium-sized kadhai (Indian high-sided wok), toast the amaranth on medium heat. Toss the grains until they are lightly browned, about 5–6 minutes. Remove the seeds from the pan and set aside.

In the same pan, add the ghee, then the peanuts and cashew nuts, and dry-roast until they darken in colour and change aroma. Remove from the pan and set aside.

Add the mustard seeds, red chilies, ginger, and green chili, in that order, and let them sputter. Next, add the onions and toss until they turn translucent, 1 minute. Add the curry leaves and give the mixture another minute to cook together.

While this mixture is cooking, thaw the peas (if using frozen) and microwave on high, for 1 minute. Add them to the pan and toss for 2 minutes.

Add the water and bring the mixture to a boil, then stir in the toasted amaranth seeds and salt to taste. Reduce the heat to a low simmer, cover the pan, and cook until the water has been absorbed and steam tunnels form, about 15 minutes, stirring every 5 minutes to prevent sticking or burning.

Test for doneness; well-cooked amaranth has a chewy texture, not crunchy.

Serve hot with the roasted peanuts and cashews and lime juice sprinkled on top.

No-Waste Charred Avocado on Toast

Vg / LW
10 minutes
Makes 2 servings

GATHER

1 tsp olive oil
1 tsp sunflower seeds
½ bell pepper, finely diced
1 green chili, finely sliced
1 tsp crushed peanuts (optional)
1 Tbsp lentil sprouts (page 86) (optional)
1 avocado
1 Tbsp sesame seeds
1 tsp lime juice
Salt to taste
Sugar to taste (optional)
2 slices bread of choice, toasted

Avocado was hard to include in this book, mainly because of how inaccessible it is for most people around the world. For centuries, avocados were a highly prized staple food in Central and South America. Today, this crop is cultivated in many areas of the world, and it is still of great value because of its water- and labour-intensive nature. Throwing this valuable fruit away simply because it has overripened should be a big NO, right? In this recipe, I share how to cook overripe mushy avocados. The trick? Pan-frying the slices not only adds flavour and crunch but also keeps this bounty of the land from ending up in the landfill.

MAKE

Place a skillet on the stove on medium-high heat. Add the olive oil and let it heat through. Add the sunflower seeds, bell peppers, sliced green chili, peanuts, and lentil sprouts (if using), in that order. Toss and roast for 1 minute. Move the mixture to the outer edges of the pan.

Cut the avocado lengthwise around the seed and separate it into 2 halves. Cup the half with the seed in the palm of your hand, seed side up. Carefully give the seed a quick smack with the sharp side of the knife, allowing the blade to embed. Twist the seed off with the knife. Slice the avocado without cutting through the peel and then scoop the flesh into the pan. The hardest part of this recipe is done.

Let the avocado slices get some char, without moving them around. Sprinkle with the sesame seeds, lime juice, salt, and sugar (if using). Scoop the charred slices out along with the bell pepper mixture and place them on toast. The best kind of avo toast there is.

#GOGREEN TIP
Avocado mouldy or smelling off? Cut off the blackened sections and compost them. Use the rest.

Dips and Dressings, Chutneys, and Condiments

Fresh Cilantro and Mint Chutney

Vg / *LW*
15 minutes
Makes 1 cup

GATHER

2 cups loosely packed cilantro leaves
   and top stems

½ cup loosely packed mint leaves
   (no stems)

3 green chilies, stems off

1 medium shallot, peeled and cut into
   chunks

3 Tbsp lime juice (approx. 1½ limes)

1 tsp salt

1 tsp sugar

1–2 Tbsp cold water for blending

Equipment
High-speed blender

This herbaceous green chutney is on weekly rotation in my mom's house. Its tangy flavour and deep chlorophyll nature add sparkle to a host of dishes. Every family and community has its own recipe, though. Variations with fresh coconut, roasted lentils, and toasted nuts are quite common and add flavours and smoothness that perk up the palate in different ways. This recipe is close to how my mom makes it. I hope you enjoy!

MAKE

Combine all the ingredients in the blender, except the water. Blend until the mixture has the consistency of a thick smoothie, 3–4 minutes. Push down the contents of the blender, scrape down the edges, and add cold water a tablespoon at a time. Blend again. Avoid overblending as the herbs may turn bitter.

Store in the fridge for up to 5 days. The mint and lime juice combination will darken the chutney as it oxidizes.

HOW TO EAT
Enjoy with Besan and Broccoli Pakoras (page 153) or Chickpea Flour Pancakes (page 165).

VARIATIONS
Looking for a creamier texture? Add 2 Tbsp roasted peanuts, cashews, or fresh coconut.

> #GOGREEN TIP
> Switch the herbs up with what you have to avoid waste. Parsley and dill add their own unique flavours to this chutney.

Roasted Peanut Chutney

GATHER

For the Chutney

1 cup unsalted peanuts, skinless and lightly roasted

1 cup yogurt (runny is better)

1 tsp cumin powder

1 tsp coriander powder

2 fresh hot green chilies, stems off

Cool water to blend

For the Tadka

1 Tbsp coconut oil

½ tsp mustard seeds

2 dried red chilies

Handful of fresh (or dried) curry leaves

Equipment

High-speed blender

I typically have a selection of chutneys stowed away in the back of my fridge. One blend in particular, with its spicy, creamy, and vibrant flavours, is a consistent favourite. That's roasted peanut chutney, a versatile condiment that makes a delicious accompaniment for a ton of different dishes; moong-lette or chickpea flour pancakes or even good ol' plain vegetables such as celery and carrots.

MAKE

For the Chutney

Blend the peanuts, yogurt, cumin, coriander, and green chilies together into a smooth mixture, about 2 minutes. Add cool water as needed. Refrigerate for up to 2 weeks.

For the Tadka

Heat the coconut oil in a pan on medium-high. Add the mustard seeds, red chilies, and curry leaves, in that order. Toss, and give the mixture 2–3 minutes to get crispy. Don't let it burn.

Pour the tadka on the peanut chutney just as you sit down to eat.

Garlicky White (Bean) Sauce

Vg / PF
15 minutes
Makes 2 cups

GATHER

Two 19 oz (540 mL) cans white beans
 (navy or Great Northern)
2 Tbsp olive oil
6 garlic cloves, finely chopped
¼ cup water (approx.)
1 tsp lemon juice
½ tsp cumin powder
½ tsp ground pepper (white or black)
½ tsp salt

This accidentally vegan, deliberately delicious white sauce came about as a delightful surprise. For years I had been researching and testing dishes that were free of dairy and wheat. It was during one such exploration that I discovered that white beans—all kinds of navy, cannellini, butter, and broad beans—make an excellent, gut-healthy and environmentally friendly substitute for dairy.

MAKE

Open the cans of beans, drain and rinse them, and set aside.

Heat a saucepan on medium heat and add the olive oil, then the garlic. Stir until the mixture is fragrant, about 45 seconds. Add the beans to the pan along with ¼ cup water. Simmer the mixture until heated through, about 4 minutes.

Remove the saucepan from the heat and scrape the mixture into a blender. Add the lemon juice, cumin, pepper, and salt, and purée. Add more water if needed, depending on the consistency you're looking for. Use less water and leave the mixture thick for a great dip. Use more water to make a delicious vegan pasta sauce.

Refrigerate for up to 1 week.

RECIPE NOTE
Cooking beans from scratch? See page 91 for how to do this.

Good Mood Dressing with Yogurt and Tahini

V
10 minutes
Makes ¾ cup

GATHER

4 Tbsp plain yogurt

2 Tbsp tahini (sesame seed paste)

1 tsp lime juice

¼ tsp cumin powder

Salt and pepper to taste

1–2 Tbsp water (approx.)

2 Tbsp chopped fresh mint (or dill) (optional)

Without a doubt, this has been one of my favourite salad dressings for as long as I can remember. The recipe features two incredibly flavourful and gut-healthy ingredients that tick all the Eating with Benefits boxes: sesame seeds and plain yogurt. What's more, this dressing is incredibly versatile, you can add a variety of herbs and spices to make it your own.

MAKE

Whisk together the yogurt, tahini, lime juice, cumin, and salt and pepper until smooth. Add 1–2 Tbsp water to thin the mixture and get the right consistency for dressing. Add some of the oil from the tahini paste for deeper flavour. Stir in the chopped herbs if using.

HOW TO EAT

Toss with your favourite salad when you're ready to eat.

VARIATIONS

Using this dressing as a dip? Skip the water and leave the consistency more viscous.

Scraptastic Orange Peel Chutney

Vg / PF
15 minutes prep +
2 hours simmering
Makes 2 cups

GATHER

1 cup orange peels, rinsed
1 cup dried dates, pits removed
1 cup water (approx.)
1 tomato, chopped
2-inch piece ginger, chopped
¼ cup sugar
1 tsp black peppercorns
1 tsp coriander seeds
1 tsp turmeric powder
½ tsp mustard powder
½ tsp salt

There are two types of chutneys: the herbaceous kind with fresh herbs, and the kind that is slow-cooked over hours to deepen the flavours and mellow the texture. In the latter, you end up with softened fruit in a tangy, sweet and sour mixture. Above all, you use one of the most underrated foods as the hero—orange peels!

MAKE

To prepare the orange peels, scrape away and discard any extra white pith, then slice them thinly in 1-inch long strips.

Combine all ingredients in a heavy-bottomed pan. Bring the mixture to a boil on medium heat, then turn down to a low simmer and cook for 2 hours. Check every 10 minutes, adding an additional ½ cup water at a time if the mixture starts to dry out. Stir occasionally.

Cool the chutney and store it in an airtight container in the fridge for up to 3 months.

HOW TO EAT
Enjoy as a dip with crackers as part of a charcuterie board. A teaspoon in your favourite marinade or in No-Waste Orange and Green Chicken Stir-Fry (page 219) adds so much flavour.

Sweet and Spicy Chili Oil

Vg / PF
30 minutes
Makes 1 cup

GATHER

¾ cup vegetable oil

4 Tbsp rice wine vinegar

½ cup chopped green and/or red chilies

2 Tbsp sesame seeds

2–3 cloves garlic, minced (optional)

1 Tbsp Sichuan peppercorns (optional)

2 Tbsp sugar

1 tsp salt

Equipment
Small glass jar with lid

I have had a jar of this spicy, sweet, totally addictive condiment sitting on my counter every week since that first summer of COVID. I make a fresh batch regularly and eat it with everything, for example, drizzled on No-Waste Charred Avocado on Toast (page 111) or with Japanese-Style Okonomiyaki (page 167). This recipe is a mash-up technique that is a combination of chili oil and chili crisp, and it comes together easily. And the flavours? Yum!

MAKE

Heat the oil and vinegar in a small saucepan over medium heat, stirring slowly as needed. Check whether the mixture is at the right temperature by dropping in a piece of chili. It should immediately sputter and rise to the surface. If it sinks, continue to heat. *Note:* Be careful when heating the oil and vinegar mixture. Don't leave the pan unattended, and guard against splashing.

Add the chopped chilies and sesame seeds, along with the garlic and Sichuan peppercorns (if using). Stir gently for 1–2 minutes.

Remove the pan from the heat and add the sugar and salt. Stir until dissolved. Let the mixture cool completely.

Store in an airtight glass jar at room temperature for up to 1 month.

Deeply Sour and Sweet
Tamarind Sauce

Vg / PF
1 hour
Makes 1 cup

GATHER

7 oz (200 g) package seedless tamarind
pulp

3 cups water (approx.)

1 cup dried dates, pitted

¼ cup brown sugar

½ tsp fennel seeds

1-inch piece ginger

Equipment
Mesh strainer with medium holes

Tamarind is the fruit of a very commonplace tropical tree—so common that despite the fruit's immunity-boosting, antioxidant, and anti-inflammatory properties, it's often overlooked, taken for granted even. Ancient wisdom in India and many other countries has long advised that people eat tamarind regularly for its nutritional properties and for its deeply sour and tangy flavour. The easiest and most flavourful way to eat this seedy, pulpy fruit is to transform it into a sauce. It refrigerates well and can be added to any number of dishes like Sweet, Sour, and Spicy Bhel Puri (page 149) and Chana Masala (page 203), as well as to marinades and other sauces.

MAKE

Mix the tamarind pulp and 1 cup water together in a heavy-bottomed saucepan and turn the heat to medium. Keep to a low simmer and cook for 30 minutes. If the mixture starts to stick to the bottom of the pan or dries out, add an additional ½ cup water at a time and stir.

After 30 minutes, strain the mixture through the mesh strainer over a bowl, pressing out all the liquid from the pulp (and seeds, if any). Pour 1 cup water on the pulpy mixture and run it through the strainer to get all the last bits of pulp.

Pour the strained liquid back into the saucepan and add the dates, sugar, fennel seeds, ginger, and another cup of water. Simmer for 20 minutes. The final consistency of the tamarind sauce should be similar to that of lumpy ketchup.

Store in an airtight jar in the refrigerator for up to 3 months.

HOW TO EAT

Mix as needed into marinades for a deep tangy flavour.

Dilute with equal ratio of water and use in Sweet, Sour, and Spicy Bhel Puri (page 149).

Turmeric Root Pickle

GATHER

4-inch piece fresh turmeric
8 small green chilies
¼ cup fresh lime juice (approx. 2 limes)
½ tsp salt

Equipment
Small glass jar with lid; a sunny windowsill

This is a simple, four-ingredient, tangy pickle that is different from the usual variety of Indian pickles. For one, it doesn't use oil or whole spices, and it is made with fresh turmeric root that has been steeped in just lime juice and salt. Turmeric is an important immunity-boosting, anti-inflammatory food. As a spice, it is often found in kitchens in its dried, powdered form. The fresh root, though, is lovely and far more flavourful than you might expect.

MAKE

Peel the turmeric root and slice it into 1-inch matchsticks. Trim the green chilies and slice them lengthwise. Use a spoon to scoop out as much of the membrane and seeds as possible.

In a separate bowl, whisk together the lime juice and salt.

Fill a glass jar with the sliced turmeric and green chilies, and pour in the lime juice mixture. Close the lid, find a sunny windowsill, and leave it there for 3 days. Loosen the lid each day to allow the gases to escape, close the lid, and repeat the next day. Shake occasionally if the turmeric looks like it's drying out.

After 3 days, store the pickle in the fridge for up to 3 months.

HOW TO EAT
Serve alongside any of the dishes in the Savoury Pan Crepe section or tucked inside a wrap or roll of your choice.

Fresh turmeric will stain your fingertips and also the chopping board. Use a half lime and a sprinkle of baking soda to scrub the colour away.

Homemade Maple Mustard

Vg / PF / LW
Overnight soaking + 10 minutes
Makes 1 cup

GATHER

½ cup black mustard seeds
¼ cup rice wine vinegar
½ tsp salt
½ tsp turmeric powder
2 Tbsp maple syrup

Equipment
Bowl; high-speed blender; small jar
with lid

Homemade mustard is an unexpectedly easy flavour bomb. Its pungent, tangy flavours do so much with little effort, and it is surprisingly easy to make. And today, with all the shortages affecting Dijon mustard, having this accessible, delicious shortcut that adds flavour in any number of ways is definitely a blessing!

MAKE

Place the mustard seeds in a bowl with the vinegar and enough water to just cover the seeds. Let them soak for at least 6 hours, ideally overnight.

Grind the seeds and the soaking liquid together in a blender. Add the salt, turmeric powder, and more water to get the consistency you prefer. *Note:* The mixture thickens over time in the fridge. Avoid over blending; leaving some of the seeds whole lends a more enjoyable, grainy texture.

Decant into a jar, add the maple syrup, and stir together. Store in the refrigerator for up to 3 months.

VARIATIONS
Got yellow mustard seeds instead of black? Use what you have. The flavour may be a little less pungent, yellow mustard seeds have a less intense flavour, but the condiment will still be delicious in the end.

Perfectly Simple Hummus

Vg / PF
15 minutes
Makes 4 servings

GATHER

1 cup boiled chickpeas (see page 91)
  (or canned chickpeas)
¼ cup olive oil
¼ cup tahini
2 garlic cloves
1 tsp lime juice (lemon juice will work
  too)
1 tsp sesame seeds
¼ cup water (approx.)
⅓ tsp salt (approx.)
Cooked chickpeas and sesame seeds,
  for garnish

Equipment
Food processor

Shortly after we were married in India, my husband and I moved to Dubai for a few years. It was there that I had my first bite of traditional hummus—a blend of sesame seeds, boiled chickpeas, and lemon juice. Since then, I've had this dip at more meals in more ways than I can remember. One thing is clear: you have not tasted hummus till you have made it yourself in your own kitchen. There's something quite timeless about dried, dormant legumes being turned into this lovely quite addictive dip.

MAKE

In a food processor, blend together the chickpeas, 3 Tbsp of the olive oil, the tahini, garlic, lime juice, and sesame seeds. Add the water a little at a time until you reach the desired, paste-y consistency. I like it just a minute before smooth; my family likes it as creamy as possible. Add salt to taste, about ⅓ tsp.

Garnish with the remaining 1 Tbsp olive oil, a few cooked chickpeas, and a sprinkle of sesame seeds.

HOW TO EAT
Serve with warm pita, bread fingers from Leftover Bread 4 Ways (page 146), crackers, or sliced veggies.

GARNISH VARIATIONS
- Browned garlic and roasted pine nuts
- Za'atar and paprika
- Dukkah-Inspired Nutty Seasoning Blend (page 131)
- Roasted red peppers and sun-dried tomatoes
- Dried mint, swirled right through

Baingan Bharta Caponata

Vg
40 minutes
Makes 4 servings

GATHER

4 Tbsp olive oil

4 garlic cloves, minced

4 cups diced (1 inch) skin-on eggplant

1 tsp coriander powder

1 tsp cumin powder

1 cup finely chopped tomatoes

½ red onion, diced

½ tsp cayenne pepper

½ tsp turmeric powder

1 Tbsp lime juice (approx. ½ lime)

Big pinch of sugar

Salt to taste

Handful of chopped basil leaves

Baingan bharta is Hindi for "eggplant mash," a dish that is a party of flavours with roasted eggplant, onions, tomatoes, and various spices. Caponata is a tangy and sweet eggplant dish with Sicilian roots. Together, my Baingan Bharta Caponata is a medley of memories that brings my Indian roots and love for Italian food together in one dish. It is a spicy and sour dish that truly shows off the unassuming eggplant as the star of the dinner table.

MAKE

Place a skillet on the stove and turn the heat to medium-high. Add the olive oil and garlic and sauté for 2 minutes. Next, add the eggplant, coriander, and cumin and continue to cook, stirring frequently, until the eggplant starts to become tender and somewhat mellow, about 10 minutes.

Add the tomatoes, onions, cayenne pepper, and turmeric and cook for another 10 minutes. Stir in the lime juice and sugar, turn the heat to medium-low, and cook until the eggplant skin has softened and the mixture is aromatic, another 15 minutes. Add salt to taste. Garnish with the basil leaves.

HOW TO EAT

Serve in the centre of the table with a sliced baguette for scooping.

Dukkah-Inspired Nutty Seasoning Blend

Vg / PF
15 minutes
Makes just under 1 cup

GATHER

1 tsp olive oil
½ cup pistachio nuts, shelled
¼ cup sesame seeds
1 Tbsp fennel seeds
2 tsp cumin seeds
2 tsp coriander seeds
2 tsp black peppercorns
½ tsp salt
Sprinkle of sugar

Equipment
Mortar and pestle (or spice grinder)

Dukkah is a wonderfully fragrant combination of roasted nuts, seeds, and spices that can be used along with, on top of, or inside a host of other dishes. The Middle-Eastern flavours of this seasoning complement most savoury dishes and add texture and crunch quite quickly. One of my favourite ways to eat this blend is stirred into to olive oil with bread for dunking.

MAKE

Place a skillet on the stove, turn the heat to medium, and add the oil. Add the pistachios and sesame seeds to the pan and gently toast for 5 minutes. Be careful not to burn the mixture. Set aside.

In the same pan, toast the fennel seeds, cumin seeds, coriander seeds, and peppercorns until the aroma changes, about 3 minutes. Set aside to cool completely.

Once everything is cool, crush and stir it all together with the salt and sugar. I prefer a mortar and pestle here because they allow me to control the texture. You could also use a spice grinder, but leave the setting at coarse. The whole bits add that distinctively warm and crunchy flavour that dukkah is famous for.

VARIATION
Swap out the pistachios for peanuts for a more economical and planet-friendly option.

My Mom's Garam Masala Blend

Vg / PF
15 minutes
Makes ½ cup

GATHER

2 Tbsp cumin seeds
8 black cardamom pods
4-inch piece of cinnamon bark
2 Tbsp black peppercorns
2 tsp whole cloves
A few small pieces of a cracked whole
 nutmeg, approx. ½ tsp

Equipment
Spice grinder

Start with whole spices and
the flavours will be deeper
and last longer.

The word *garam* in Hindi/Urdu translates to "hot" and can mean two things: straight-out-of-the-oven hot or "Yikes, this is spicy." This leads to confusion in the English language because so many of us—and it may be a cultural thing—refer to spicy food as "hot" food.

This brings me to garam masala, i.e. a "hot blend of spices." It seems like every family, community, and region in India has its own version. This particular combination is inspired by my mom's version. It's the one I grew up knowing and loving. I hope you enjoy it too!

MAKE

Place a skillet on the stove and turn the heat to medium. Add the whole spices, in the order listed, to the pan to toast. Toss gently until fragrant, about 2 minutes. Allow the spices to cool completely.

Grind the spices in a spice grinder until very fine. Store the garam masala in an airtight glass jar for up to 6 months.

RECIPE NOTE
Looking for a quick fix? Buy single-origin ground spices in small quantities and mix them using the same ratio.

Sun-Fermented Vegetables (Kanji)

Vg / LW
3–5 days
Makes 10 cups

GATHER

5–6 medium-sized carrots

2 small beets

1 small turnip

1 small radish

Rind of a ¼ mini watermelon, approx.
 ½ cup watermelon rinds,

3 Tbsp black mustard seeds

1 tsp Himalayan pink salt (or regular
 salt)

10 cups water

Equipment

Large mixing bowl; mortar and pestle
or spice grinder; multiple small jars with
lids; muslin cloth (optional)

Kanji is a fermented drink popular in northern India. Come January, you'll see it on windowsills and porches around Punjab, where jars of vegetables are left out in the sun to ferment and develop deep flavours and probiotic richness. Made with warming ingredients, kanji makes an excellent immunity-boosting aperitif, and the crunchy vegetables are great for snacking too. I remember light brown ceramic jars packed with purple carrots lined up in a corner in my parents' kitchen in New Delhi when I was a child. They were a reminder that foggy winter days were around the corner. Today, the brown ceramic jars are gone, but the tradition and techniques continue.

MAKE

Rinse and peel the vegetables. For tender radishes, leave the skin on and scrub. For the watermelon rinds, peel and discard the green skin and use the white part only.

Slice all the vegetables and watermelon rinds into long, thin batons about 3 inches long, almost like fries. You should have about 4 cups sliced vegetables in total. Set them aside in a large bowl.

Crush the mustard seeds a few times with a mortar and pestle. If you're using a spice grinder, set it to pulse and stop while the seeds are still coarse.

Add the crushed mustard seeds, salt, and water to the bowl of vegetables and stir well. Divide the vegetables and liquid among your glass jars. Cover them loosely with lids or muslin cloth, and keep the jars in a sunny spot for 3–4 days. If you live in an area where the sun is unpredictable, like I do, find a warm spot in your kitchen and allow the kanji to ferment an extra couple of days. Stir the mixture every day with a clean wooden spoon; replace the lids (loosely) or cloth before putting the jars back in the sun.

The kanji is ready when it tastes sour; the sourness indicates that the drink has fermented.

Refrigerate and enjoy within 10 days.

RECIPE NOTE

Take care not to over ferment the drink. If the fermentation process does not go well, kanji can go bad. If the jars smell rancid, the texture is slimy, or there's pale-coloured mould on the surface, throw it out and start again.

HOW TO EAT

Serve as an aperitif. The vegetables are often eaten separately as a crunchy topping on salads, or with Calcutta-Style Kathi Rolls (page 227).

#GOGREEN TIP
Make the last-days-of-summer veggies last longer— ferment them! Make kanji.

Fermentation is quite popular in India in a variety of ways. Kanji in particular is known for its gut-healthy, probiotic-rich qualities that boost the belly and the brain.

Crunchy Oat Topping

Vg / PF
20 minutes
Makes 1 cup

GATHER

2 Tbsp olive oil

¼ cup whole millet grains, rinsed and drained

½ tsp salt

1 cup unflavoured quick oats or instant oats

1 tsp brown sugar

1 tsp smoked paprika or any mild red chili powder

Some foods work wonderfully as companions. With its crisp texture and burst of flavour, this Crunchy Oat Topping complements other foods and helps them shine. I often make a double batch, cool it, and store it on the kitchen counter, ready to eat in boundless ways; sprinkle it on hummus (page 127), Keema Aloo Shepherd's Pie (page 207), or even mac and cheese or a salad. (Topping pictured on page 130.)

MAKE

Place a skillet on the stove on medium-high heat. Add 1 Tbsp of the olive oil and allow it to heat through. Next, add the millet grains and toast for 2–3 minutes. Turn the heat down to medium and continue to toss the grains. Add the salt.

Roast the mixture for 10–12 minutes, allowing the millet grains to fully cook through. Taste-test a couple of grains; the texture should be crunchy, not chewy.

Add the remaining 1 Tbsp of oil and the oats, and cook for another 5–7 minutes. At the last minute, add the sugar and paprika, and toss. Dried red chili powder like paprika burns quickly, so turn the heat off quickly once you've added it.

Toasties and Snacks

Roasted Chickpeas

Vg / PF
20 minutes + 5 minutes of rest
Makes 4 cups

GATHER

Two 19 oz (540 mL) cans chickpeas
   (or freshly cooked chickpeas, roasted
   for a few minutes less)
3 Tbsp olive oil
Salt to taste
Big pinch of paprika and sugar

Equipment
Baking pan; silicone mat (optional)

Roasted chickpeas are a quick, crispy snack that is quite easy to make. These little nuggets of goodness roast quickly and can be stored for weeks on the kitchen counter. Personally, I like them with simple flavours like salt and red chili powder, but the possibilities are endless. You can get creative and try any number of seasoning and spice blends. The best part? It's not just the crunchiness; chickpeas are good for us and great for the planet.

MAKE

Preheat the oven to 425°F. Rinse the canned chickpeas and allow them to sit in a colander to drain the liquid. Prepare the baking pan with a silicone mat (if using) and spread the chickpeas out. Drizzle the olive oil on the legumes, sprinkle salt over them, and toss.

Roast the chickpeas in the oven for 20–25 minutes. Watch carefully past the 15-minute mark; chickpeas go from brown to burnt quite quickly.

Take the pan out and toss the still-hot chickpeas with the paprika and sugar. Chickpeas will get crispier as they cool, so allow them to sit on the counter for a few minutes before you check for texture. Once they are cooled, store them in an airtight container at room temperature for up to 1 month.

HOW TO EAT

Serve as a snack, as a crunchy topping on salad leaves, or with whole grains.

VARIATION

Add a sprinkle of My Mom's Garam Masala Blend (page 133) after taking the pan out of the oven, for a punchier snack.

Quick-Roasted Lotus Seeds (Makhane)

Vg / *PF*
15 minutes
Makes 4 cups

GATHER

3 tsp olive oil
4 cups makhane
Salt to taste
½ tsp paprika
Big pinch of sugar

Equipment
Large, heavy-bottomed kadhai or deep skillet

Makhane, also known as popped lotus seeds, are the epitome of food for both people and planet. I grew up eating makhane every day, but it was only when I was researching this book that I truly understood the value of this nutritionally dense food. The seeds are hand harvested from the Indian lotus flower, a crop that has flourished for generations, with very little human intervention. In the last 20 years, this sustainably grown crop has become quite vital for parts of northeastern India and is bringing revenue and abundance into what was previously a struggling region.

What does it taste like? Makhane have an airy yet chewy texture that makes them suitable for any number of dishes, even curries and desserts. My favourite way of enjoying this delicious food is as a snack. (Recipe pictured on page 140.)

MAKE

Heat the kadhai on medium-high and add the oil and allow it to heat through. Add the makhane and roast for 7–8 minutes, tossing every 20–30 seconds. The seeds will char if they're allowed to settle on high heat so keep them moving occasionally. Add salt to taste and continue to roast for another 2–3 minutes.

Once the makhane have lightly browned, add the paprika and sugar. Turn the heat off and toss a couple of times. **Note:** both paprika and sugar burn quickly so be vigilant once you've sprinkled them in. Taste for seasoning and texture. The makhane should have a lightly crispy outer layer and be fluffy on the inside.

Cool completely and store in an airtight glass container at room temperature for up to 1 week.

Leftover Bread 4 Ways

Food waste is an enormous burden on our wallets and also on the planet's resources. Leftover bread is one of the largest contributors to this mountain of waste around the world. Not only does this result in more bread in landfills, the waste also includes the water, resources, and land used to grow the grains for that bread.

So what can we do? To start, buy only what we need. And then eat it. If there's too much bread that we can't get to in a reasonable time, give it to a neighbour (or a food bank that accepts baked goods) or freeze it.

Freezing is the easiest way to extend the life of the loaf. Thaw frozen bread when needed and use it in any number of ways: bread pudding, French toast, bread crumbs, and more. Here are four creative options (and there's a fifth recipe at the end of the book, a decadent, sweet way to finish a meal).

Note: these recipes are made using leftover bread. The ingredient quantities vary depending on the type of bread being used. I suggest you try the recipes out, eye ball the seasoning—Andaaze Se—add more (or less) of what you need and adjust the time accordingly.

CROUTONS

GATHER

Olive oil
Salt
Finely minced garlic
Black pepper
Leftover bread

Equipment
Large bowl; baking sheet

Making croutons is remarkably easy because you can use any type of bread—multi-grain, cheese, even gluten-free will work—and then customize with flavour and spices that feel right in the moment. Use them to add pep and crunch to your next salad or soup.

MAKE

Preheat the oven to 350°F. In a large mixing bowl, stir together the olive oil, salt, garlic, and black pepper. Cube the bread and gently toss it in the oil mixture. Lay the cubes out on a baking sheet and bake until golden and crispy, about 15 minutes. Let the croutons cool completely and store them in a glass jar for up to 2 weeks.

Note: Baking times for different breads may vary. Experiment with what works for you and your oven.

*Clockwise from top left:
Crackers, Upma, Croutons,
Bread Fingers*

CRACKERS

GATHER

Leftover bread slices
Olive oil
Dukkah-Inspired Nutty Seasoning
  Blend (page 131)

Equipment
Rolling pin; baking sheet

Confession time: our go-to dinner on the go is often a DIY char-cuterie board. Homemade crackers are always a great option, but they're usually really cumbersome to make. Not these ones made from leftover bread!

MAKE

Preheat the oven to 350°F. Prepare the slices of bread by cutting the sides away. (Use white bread for best results.) Reserve the sides to make Sticky and Sweet Bread Fingers (below). Use a rolling pin to roll out the slices as thin as you can. Cut them into quarters and lay them out on a baking sheet. Drizzle the olive oil and sprinkle the dukkah seasoning overtop. (Alternatively, salt and black pepper are also delicious here.) Using the back of a spoon, press the seasoning down on the bread. The olive oil will also help the topping stick. Bake for 10 minutes. Cool and store in an airtight container for up to 1 week.

STICKY AND SWEET BREAD FINGERS

GATHER

Leftover bread crusts and sides
Olive oil
Maple syrup
Sesame seeds

Equipment
Rolling pin; baking sheet

It's the bread butts and sides that are always left over, right? Here's what you can do with these bits of bread.

MAKE

Slice the leftover crusts and sides into finger-width pieces. In a large skillet, add the olive oil and heat through on medium. Fry the bread crusts for 3–4 minutes, tossing regularly. Drizzle the maple syrup on the crusts (watch out for sputtering) and sprinkle the sesame seeds overtop. Toss and continue to cook. Turn the heat down if needed to avoid burning.

If you're using multi-grain bread, the crusts are cooked through when they are an even, sticky almond colour. With white bread, the crusts are done when they are a pale brown colour.

Eat while still warm, though these sticky and sweet bread sides are pretty great once cool, too.

NO-WASTE GOLDEN BREAD UPMA

V / LW
25 minutes
Makes 4 servings

GATHER

1 Tbsp ghee

1 tsp mustard seeds

1 tsp turmeric powder

1 green chili, finely chopped

1 cup finely chopped red onions

1 cup diced (½ inch) sweet potatoes

½ cup green peas (frozen or fresh)

1 tsp cane sugar

½ tsp hing powder

Salt to taste

1 Tbsp olive oil

2 handfuls of curry leaves (approx. 20)

2 Tbsp sesame seeds

6 cups cubed, stale, days-old bread

½ tsp red chili powder

⅓ tsp black pepper

1 Tbsp lime juice (approx. ½ lime)

½ cup chopped cilantro leaves

½ cup coarsely chopped, unsalted,
   roasted peanuts

Equipment
Kadhai or large skillet

Use any kind of bread for upma, including whole-grain, gluten-free, or challah. Adjust the oil and spices according to the texture of the bread.

This recipe is inspired by a traditional South Indian dish that is normally made with semolina flour. In my version, I use slightly stale, dried-up old bread. Cube and sizzle-fry, and then toss with mustard seeds, turmeric, green chilies, onions, hing, and curry leaves. Enjoy!

MAKE

If using frozen peas, soak them in boiling-hot water for 5 minutes, or microwave for 2 minutes.

Heat the ghee in a kadhai or large skillet and let it melt. Turn the heat to medium, add the mustard seeds, and sauté for 1 minute. Add the turmeric powder and let the colours darken. Next, add the green chilies, onions, sweet potatoes, and peas, and toss. Add the sugar, the hing, and salt to taste. Cook this mixture for 5 minutes on medium heat and let the onions and sweet potatoes soak up the flavour of the spices.

Push this mixture to the outer edges of the pan and add the oil to the centre of the pan. Add the curry leaves, sesame seeds, and cubed bread, in that order. Sprinkle in the chili powder and black pepper and toss the bread together with the spices. Continue to toss occasionally and cook on medium-high heat for 5 minutes.

Add the lime juice and toss again. Taste and adjust the salt. The dish is ready when the diced bread has turned golden and some pieces have a gentle char on them.

Garnish with the cilantro and roasted peanuts, and serve warm.

HOW TO EAT

Serve as stuffing on the side or as a weeknight dinner when the fridge is empty but there's bread in the freezer.

Sweet, Sour, and Spicy Bhel Puri

Vg / PF
15 minutes
Makes 6 small bowls

Bhel puri is a classic Indian street snack that is often served in a paper cone or on dried banana leaves. I remember getting a plate of this crunchy snack as a child on the way back from school, from the cart down the street from my grandparents' house in South Delhi. Since then I've eaten bhel thousands (!!) of times and each time it's just a little different.

It's quite possible there are a million recipes out there, but the most successful ones use a combination of textures and sauces that bring sweet, spicy, sour, crunchy, and fresh together. In my version, I add quinoa puffs and chopped apple that really bring India and Canada together in a bowl.

GATHER

For the Dressing

2 Tbsp Deeply Sour and Sweet Tamarind Sauce (page 123) (or 3 Tbsp jarred tamarind paste)

2 Tbsp Fresh Cilantro and Mint Chutney (page 114) (or 2 Tbsp lime juice)

2 green chilies, finely sliced

1 Tbsp maple syrup (or honey)

⅓ tsp black rock salt

⅓ tsp red chili powder

⅓ tsp cumin powder

For the Dry Bhel Puri Mix

8.8 oz (250 g) bag dry bhel puri mix, or make your own with:

1 cup puffed rice (murmura)

1 cup puffed quinoa

¼ cup roasted peanuts, roughly chopped

¼ cup small broken pieces of matthi (whole wheat crackers)

For the Salad

½ cup finely diced tomatoes

½ cup finely diced apples

½ cup chopped cilantro (tender top stems and leaves only)

⅓ cup finely chopped red onions

¼ cup fine chickpea noodles (sev)

MAKE

In a large glass bowl, mix the dressing ingredients together and set aside. Dilute the Deeply Sour and Sweet Tamarind Sauce with equal quantity water as needed.

Set up your station and prepare the rest of the ingredients as listed. Keep the dry bhel puri mix and the salad ingredients separate until you're ready to toss everything together.

When you're ready to eat, mix together the dry bhel puri mix and the salad ingredients. Add the dressing and use a soft-edged paddle to toss and gently mix everything together.

Serve in individual bowls. Finish with a generous sprinkle of chickpea noodles, or sev (buy them separately if not included in the dry bhel puri mix). Eat straightaway.

RECIPE NOTES

Using jarred tamarind paste for your dressing? The consistency may not be as expected. Add 1–2 Tbsp water to dilute it (like thin ketchup) before adding the remaining dressing ingredients.

Puffed rice hard to find? Replace it with unsweetened Rice Krispies cereal.

If you're using a prepackaged dry bhel puri mix, it may come with its own variation of the sauce.

#GOGREEN TIP

If your puffed rice is past its best-before date, place it in a bowl and microwave on high for 30–45 seconds. Toss, let cool, and use as needed for dry bhel puri mix. You can use this technique to freshen soggy crackers and cookies too.

Stuff on Toast

Stuff on toast makes an excellent meal any time of the day, whether it's hurried afternoons, dinner on the go, or, like in my home, when everyone wants something different.

Here are my two favourite options: sprouted lentil salad on toast, or Indian-Style Bruschetta; and not-baked beans that are cooked in a pressure cooker until soft. It's what my dad could eat for breakfast or dinner any day of the week. And I can too!

INDIAN-STYLE BRUSCHETTA

GATHER

Lentil sprouts (page 86)
1–2 tsp lime juice
Salt
Diced tomatoes
Chopped cilantro
Chopped red onions
Toast of choice

Sprouts are incredibly nutritious kitchen superheroes. They teach us that as long as we have a bag of dried, whole lentils, we can have access to fresh and delicious food, even in times of restrictions and shortages. This bruschetta uses moong lentil bean sprouts (see page 86) in a fresh salad tossed with chopped tomatoes, cilantro, and red onions.

MAKE

Toss the sprouts with a squeeze of lime, salt, diced tomatoes, chopped cilantro, and chopped onions. Adjust the seasoning to taste. Layer the salad on your toast of your choice, and enjoy.

NOT-BAKED BEANS

GATHER

1 Tbsp olive oil

2 bay leaves

1 tsp fennel seeds

1 heaping cup white navy beans, soaked overnight, or two 19 oz (540 mL) cans white beans, drained and rinsed

½ tsp red chili powder

¼ tsp black pepper

½ cup jarred tomato sauce

1 Tbsp Homemade Maple Mustard (page 125)

¼ cup apple cider vinegar

¼ cup maple syrup

2 cups water

Salt to taste

Toast of choice

Equipment

Instant Pot

MAKE

Turn the Instant Pot to sauté mode, add the oil, and let it heat for a couple of minutes. Add the bay leaves and fennel seeds and sauté for 10–15 seconds. Next, add the remaining ingredients in the order they are listed, allowing time to stir each one in. Put the lid on the pressure cooker.

If you are using soaked beans, cook on high pressure for 35 minutes, then do a natural pressure release for 10 minutes. For canned beans, cook on high pressure for 6 minutes, then natural pressure release for 5 minutes.

Once the pressure has been released, open the lid and stir everything together. Mash a few beans with the back of a spoon while they are still hot. Like many bean-forward dishes, this one thickens overnight. The legumes will absorb liquid and release flavour. Tons of flavour.

Serve warm on toast.

Refrigerate for up to 1 week.

Besan and Broccoli Pakoras

Vg | PF | FF
45 minutes
Makes 6 servings

GATHER

1 cup chickpea flour (besan)
2 Tbsp rice flour
1 cup finely chopped broccoli (stems, leaves, and all)
1 Tbsp finely chopped ginger
½ tsp turmeric powder
½ tsp cumin powder
¼ tsp carom seeds (ajwain)
1 tsp coriander powder
½ tsp cayenne pepper
¼ tsp freshly ground black pepper
1 cup water (approx.)
½ tsp salt (or to taste)
Handful of chopped cilantro
4 Tbsp olive oil (approx.)

VARIATIONS

Swap out the broccoli for other finely chopped veggies like cabbage, carrots, or whatever you have wilting away in the back of the fridge.

#GOGREEN TIP

If you pan-fry often and are aiming for a no-waste kitchen, set aside a small tea towel or two to blot excess oil. The oil stains are hard to get out of reusable materials so reserve these to use for other fried foods and wash them regularly.

Pakoras are crispy, spiced nuggets that are wildly popular and often deep-fried. In my version you can pan-fry and add any kind of vegetable—cauliflower, fenugreek leaves, spinach, or even plain old potato—to the batter and people will still fall in love. My favourite way to eat pakoras is alongside a cup of masala chai on a rainy afternoon in my mom's home. But tucked in between a chapatti topped with pickled red onions while I'm rushing to pick up the kids will also do. These pakoras are also delicious stirred into Tangy Besan and Yogurt Kadhi (page 205).

MAKE

Combine the chickpea flour, rice flour, broccoli, ginger, and spices and toss together. Add ½ cup water at a time, and whisk to blend together. The desired consistency of pakora batter is quite thick, like a smooth paste, and should require about 1 cup water. Mix in the salt and chopped cilantro. Taste and adjust the seasoning if needed.

Heat a small skillet on medium. Add the oil; enough to cover the bottom of the pan. Heat until there is a shimmer on the surface of the oil. Check if the oil is ready for the pakora batter by dropping a tiny piece of batter in. It should sputter and float.

Scoop 1 tsp of batter at a time into the pan. Cook 5–6 nuggets at a time, depending on the size of the pan. Fry for 2 minutes, and then flip over and fry for another minute or two on the other side. Test the first pakora by taking it out and slicing into it. It should be golden and crispy on the outside and cooked all the way through. If the colour is golden but the batter is still raw inside, lower the heat slightly and try again. Pakora-making is a life skill and once you've got the hang of it, eating vegetables will be a breeze.

Remove the pakoras from the oil to drain on a tea towel, and cook the remaining batter. Avoid overcrowding the pan, and add more oil as needed.

Serve hot with Fresh Cilantro and Mint Chutney (page 114).

Street-Style Bombay Sandwich

V
30 minutes
Makes 4 hefty sandwiches

GATHER

2 medium whole potatoes, boiled till
    fork-tender

2 medium tomatoes

2 medium red onions

1 English cucumber (or another variety)

Butter, softened to room-temperature

1 cup grated cheese, any medium-hard
    variety will do

6 Tbsp Fresh Cilantro and Mint
    Chutney (approx.) (page 114)

Black rock salt

12 slices plain white bread (or any other
    bread)

2 tsp oil for each sandwich

VARIATION

Swap out a vegetable or two for cooked,
mashed chickpeas. Use the back of a
spoon to mash them in a bowl, and then
spread them on the bread slice.

#GOGREEN TIP
To conserve energy, boil 5 potatoes instead of 2. Refrigerate the extra 3 and
add them to fritters or the pakora recipe
on page 153.

I have a weakness for sandwiches. It's the combination of layers
and textures, and how everything can come together in one juicy
bite, that really makes them enjoyable. What makes this sandwich even more special is that it's made with simple-to-find,
easy-to-afford ingredients like boiled potato, sliced tomato,
onion, and cucumber. To top it off, the popping flavours of black
salt and cilantro chutney make this an unforgettable sandwich.

MAKE

Slice the boiled potatoes, tomatoes, cucumber, and onions into
¼-inch slices. Set up your sandwich station: sliced veggies, butter,
cheese, chutney, and black rock salt.

To start assembling, butter one side of each bread slice, then spread
1 tsp chutney on each buttered side. Now start layering in this order:

- Bread slice, chutney side up
- Sliced onion
- Sliced tomato
- 1 Tbsp grated cheese
- Bread slice, chutney side down
- ½ tsp chutney spread on top of the bread slice
- Sliced cucumber
- Sliced boiled potato
- Sprinkle of black rock salt
- Bread slice with chutney side down

Repeat with the remaining bread and sliced veggies. You should
end up with 4 sandwiches. Set aside.

Place a skillet on the stove on medium heat. Drizzle a little oil into
the pan. When it's hot, gently lower 1 sandwich (2 if they fit comfortably) into the pan. Cook for 3 minutes on each side, pressing
down with a spatula to squish the layers together, until golden and
crisp. Repeat with all 4 sandwiches.

Cut the sandwiches in half and eat while still warm.

Toasties and Snacks **155**

Nothing Faux about This Veggie Burger

Vg / PF / FF
30 minutes
Makes 4 patties

GATHER

14 oz (398 mL) can black beans, drained and rinsed

14 oz (398 mL) can chickpeas, drained and rinsed

½ cup red onions, diced

4 cloves garlic, finely chopped

¼ cup chopped, loosely packed cilantro leaves

2 Tbsp chopped cilantro stems

1 tsp coriander powder

½ tsp cumin powder

½ tsp black pepper

½ tsp red chili powder (or paprika for less heat)

½ cup cooked rice (leftover works well)

2 Tbsp chickpea flour

1 Tbsp chia seeds

1 tsp lime juice

½ tsp salt (approx.)

2 Tbsp oil (approx.)

Equipment

Food processor or blender; mixing bowl

Faux meat is trending right now, and it may even have pride of place on menus around the world, but IMHO beans, legumes, and veggies shouldn't really be processed to taste or look like meat. Seems like a lot of bother for food that is delicious just the way it is. Like this no-waste, bean-forward, freezer-friendly veggie burger that is made with mostly accessible, pantry foods. The perfectly crispy exterior and juicy inside leaves all the other burgers far behind.

MAKE

In a food processor or blender, add the black beans, chickpeas, onions, garlic, cilantro leaves and stems, coriander powder, cumin, black pepper, and chili powder, and process until the mixture has a coarse texture. Transfer to a bowl, add the cooked rice, chickpea flour, chia seeds, lime juice, and salt, and mash together until evenly mixed. Taste and adjust the seasoning if needed.

Let the mixture stand for 10 minutes and then check for consistency. If it's still wet, add another tsp of chia seeds or chickpea flour and mix. The amount you need may vary depending on a variety of factors: the moisture in the vegetables and beans, or even how warm the day is where you are.

Divide the mixture and shape into 4 large patties. Pack them tightly.

Heat a skillet over medium-high heat. Add a drizzle of oil and swirl it around. There should be sufficient oil to just coat the bottom of the pan. Place the patties in the skillet and cook for 4–6 minutes per side till the exterior is light golden and looks crispy. Avoid overcrowding the pan. Serve warm, refrigerate for up to 1 week, or freeze for up to 6 months.

HOW TO EAT

As a burger on buns of your choice with lettuce, onions, and a smear of Homemade Maple Mustard (page 125).

Gujarati-Style Fermented, Baked Rice and Lentil Cake (Handvo)

V / PF / FF
4 hours soaking +
overnight fermentation +
45 minutes
Makes one 9 × 5 loaf pan

GATHER

1 cup short-grain white rice

½ cup white urad daal (black gram, skinless)

½ cup chana daal (yellow split chickpeas)

1 cup yogurt

1 tsp turmeric

1 tsp salt (approx.)

2 cups grated veggies (e.g., zucchini, carrots, cabbage)

½ cup loosely packed fresh fenugreek leaves (optional)

2 Tbsp grated apple (Royal Gala or another sweet variety)

2 tsp sugar

1 tsp finely chopped ginger

1 Tbsp lemon juice

¼ tsp hing powder

¼ tsp Kashmiri chili powder

3 Tbsp olive oil

1 tsp mustard seeds

3–4 dried whole red chiles

1 Tbsp finely chopped green chilies (optional)

10 curry leaves (2 sprigs)

1 Tbsp white sesame seeds

1 tsp baking powder

½ tsp baking soda

Equipment

Multiple bowls for fermentation; food processor; tea towel; loaf cake pan

Snacks are an important ingredient for joy. And not just any snacks, it's the spicy, crispy, crackly ones like this Gujarati *handvo* cake. This handvo cake is inspired by the street food of western India and is made with fermented rice and lentils that bring big flavour and all the nutritional advantages of fermentation. The savoury cake is made with grated veggies and spices and then baked in a loaf pan.

Don't be put off by the time it takes to ferment the batter; it's mostly hands-free. This showstopper of a dish comes together with all the Eating with Benefits strategies yet uses steps that are easy to replicate in homes around the world. So much to love here!

MAKE

Combine the rice, urad daal, and chana daal, then rinse and soak for 4 hours. Drain the water and use a food processor to blend the mixture into a coarse paste. Avoid adding water while blending. Test for texture by rubbing the grains between your thumb and fingers; the batter should feel slightly grainy but not lumpy. Pour it into a large mixing bowl and stir in the yogurt, turmeric, and ½ tsp of the salt. Cover the bowl with a dish towel and set it aside in a dark, warm space overnight, about 10–12 hours. This time will allow the batter to ferment. Set a timer for yourself so you don't forget about what's underneath the dish towel.

The next morning, you should be able to see small bubbles in the mixture. Sometimes the bubbles are not visible, and that's okay. Add the grated veggies, fenugreek leaves (if using), and grated apple, along with the sugar, ginger, lemon juice, hing, chili powder, and the remaining ½ tsp salt. Mix well, taste, adjust the salt if needed, and then set aside.

Preheat the oven to 375°F.

Heat the oil in a small saucepan on medium-high. Add the mustard seeds, crushed red chilies, green chillies (if using), and curry leaves, in that order. Allow the seeds and leaves to crackle. Finally, add the sesame seeds and stir for 10 seconds. Remove the pan from the heat and stir this tadka mixture into the batter. Add the baking powder and baking soda. The handvo cake batter is ready.

Grease the loaf cake pan with a drizzle of oil and wipe it around using your fingers. Pour the handvo batter in, smooth the top with the back of a spoon and then bake for 30 minutes. Check if the cake is done by inserting a thin knife into the centre. It should come out clean.

Let the handvo cool, but not entirely, then loosen the sides using a knife and pop the savoury cake out. Crispy, crackly, showstopper for joy, for sure!

RECIPE NOTE
A well-made handvo is soft inside but the top layer is crispy.

HOW TO EAT
Serve warm with Fresh Cilantro and Mint Chutney (page 114) and a salad of your choice, or as a snack when you have company over.

COOKING HACK
Double batch this recipe and freeze what you will not be eating in a few days. Thaw and reheat for a minute in the microwave on high.

VARIATIONS
Swap out the zucchini for another summer squash or carrots.

Savoury Pan Crepes

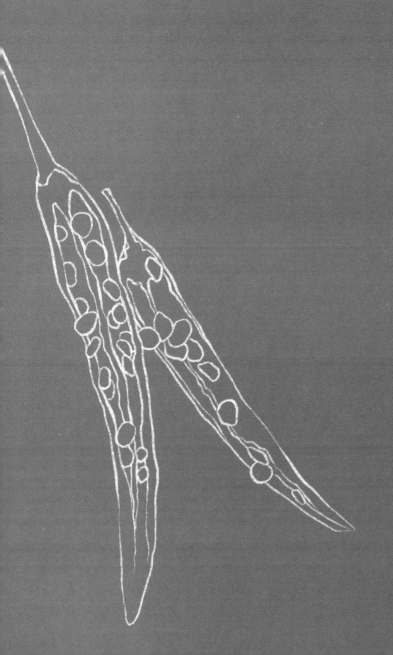

Chickpea Flour Pancakes (Puda)

Vg / PF
30 minutes + batter resting time
Makes 4 pancakes

GATHER

1 cup chickpea flour

⅓ cup rice flour

¼ cup finely chopped red onions

1 tsp coriander powder

½ tsp cumin powder

½ tsp chili powder

¼ tsp turmeric powder

¼ tsp black pepper

1½ cups water

¼ cup finely diced peppers, any colour (optional)

¼ cup chopped cilantro (optional)

1 small green chili, finely sliced (optional)

1 tsp baking powder

½ tsp salt (approx.)

4 tsp oil (approx.)

Equipment
Mixing bowl

I can eat these savoury, crispy, totally delicious pancakes straight out of the pan, that's how good they are! While I grew up eating them for breakfast, they are hearty enough to enjoy any time of day, especially when served with a light salad or chopped veggies and quick-pickled onions on the side.

MAKE

Whisk together the flours, onions, coriander, cumin, chili powders, turmeric, and black pepper in a mixing bowl. Add the water ¼ cup at a time and continue whisking. Any lumps can be mashed away on the side of the bowl. The final consistency of the batter should be thin, as if for crepes. Mix in the peppers and cilantro (if using), baking powder, and salt (start with ½ tsp and adjust to taste). Set the mixture aside for 20 minutes.

Place a heavy-bottomed skillet on medium heat. Add 1 tsp oil and swirl it around. Once you see the oil shimmer, it is ready. Pour in 3 Tbsp of batter and tilt the pan to swirl the batter around to get even thinness and a circular shape. Let the pancake sit on medium heat until you see bubbles coming up around the edges, about 3–4 minutes. The crepe is ready to flip when it looks a little crispy on the edges and comes away from the pan. Don't fight it if it doesn't come away easily; another 30 seconds in the pan and a tiny drizzle of oil should do it. Flip and brown the pancake on the other side, 2 minutes.

Repeat with the rest of the batter; it should make 4 pancakes.

Eat hot with any of the dips or chutneys (page 112), fresh greens, and pickled veggies from the Sun-Fermented Kanji (page 135).

RECIPE NOTES

Chickpea flour is a hearty, fibre-rich flour, and as a result these pancakes take a little longer to cook than those made with all-purpose flour. Allow time to cook the pancake thoroughly for the flavours to develop. The pancake edges should darken and get crispy.

Making ahead? These crepes can be prepared the day before. Wrap them in a tea towel and refrigerate. Reheat with a drizzle of oil in a pan on medium heat.

Japanese-Style Okonomiyaki

V | PF | LW
40 minutes + batter resting time
Makes 4 servings

GATHER

4 cups very finely shredded Savoy or
  other green cabbage (approx. ½ small
  head)

1 cup chopped darker leafy greens
  (e.g., Swiss chard or kale)

1 cup chopped green onions

⅔ tsp salt (approx.)

1 cup instant oats

1 cup rice flour

4 eggs

4 Tbsp yogurt

4 Tbsp room-temperature water

4 tsp olive oil

Equipment

Mixing bowls; ½-cup measure

HOW TO EAT

Serve with a generous drizzle of naturally fermented soy sauce, a big heaping
salad, and steamed rice on the side. Serve
alongside a yogurt and mayo dip made
by stirring together an equal amount of
yogurt and mayo with Sweet and Spicy
Chili Oil (page 122) to taste.

TOPPING VARIATIONS

- Quick-pickled onions + long-sliced
  ginger + sprinkle of sesame seeds
- Chili paste + Kewpie (Japanese-
  style) mayo
- Microgreens + sesame seeds +
  yogurt and mayo dip

My love for this pantry-forward, crispy, frittata-like Japanese
pancake is deep, partly because of the flavours, but mainly
because it showcases one of my favourite vegetables of all time:
cabbage. This leafy vegetable is often taken for granted because
it grows easily, uses very few resources (especially when compared with lettuce), and when wrapped in a tea towel, it can
last for months in the fridge. Months! Above all, cabbage is also
nutrition rich *and* gut healthy. But despite this ease and glory,
cabbage is widely considered a wrinkly, stinky vegetable. Not in
this dish—this okonomiyaki-like pancake brings the glorious
cabbage to life.

MAKE

In a large mixing bowl, toss the shredded cabbage, chopped greens,
green onions, and half of the salt. Set aside for 15 minutes to allow
the leaves release some of their moisture.

Add the instant oats, the remaining salt, and rice flour and combine gently.

In another bowl, whisk together the eggs, yogurt, and water. Pour
this mixture into the cabbage mixture and gently combine. *Note:*
Unlike most pancake batters, this mixture looks unformed at the
beginning. If it looks too dry and doesn't come together when
cooking, let it sit for another 10 minutes.

Heat a stainless steel skillet over medium heat. Add 1 tsp olive oil
and swirl it around to heat through. Use a ½-cup measure to scoop
the cabbage mixture into the skillet. Flatten gently with the back of
the measuring cup to ½-inch thickness. The cabbage may not feel
cohesive at first, but it will bind together as the eggs cook.

Cook until the edges start to brown, 3–4 minutes. Turn the heat
down to low if needed. Flip the pancake, add a drizzle of oil around
the edges, and cook until the other side browns evenly too, another
3–4 minutes. Remove the pancake to a plate.

Wipe the skillet in between pancakes and repeat with the remaining
mixture, adding more oil as needed.

Daal Moong-lette

Vg / PF
6 hours soaking + 30 minutes cooking
Makes 8–10 pancakes

GATHER

2 cups dried yellow split lentils (moong daal)

1-inch piece ginger, chopped

1 green chili, chopped

¾ cup water (approx.)

¼ cup finely diced onion

2 Tbsp chopped cilantro leaves and top stems

1 tsp salt

6 tsp olive oil, or another vegetable oil

Equipment

Grinder or blender; mixing bowl; kitchen towel; ¼-cup measure

I call yellow moong daal the gateway lentil. It's an easy introduction to the world of lentils for those who are new to these nutritional and environmental superheroes. Yellow moong daal, in particular, is easy on the tummy and cooks in a fraction of the time (less than 20 minutes) required for many other lentils. In addition, one of my favourite ways to eat this lentil is not in a soupy bowl but as a savoury, super-fluffy, easy-to-cook omelette that I call a moong-lette.

MAKE

Rinse the lentils 2–3 times until the water runs clear. Soak them in 4 cups water for 6 hours, or overnight.

Discard the soaking water and use a grinder or blender to blend the soaked lentils with the ginger and green chili. Add ¼ cup of the water, if needed, to blend into a smooth paste. Scrape the sides of the mixer jar with a spatula and blend again until the texture is creamy and fluffy.

Transfer the moong daal paste to a large mixing bowl. Add the onions, cilantro, salt, and approximately ½ cup water to make a medium-thick batter. Set aside.

To make the moong-lette, heat a skillet on high. Once the pan is hot, turn the heat to low, splash a drop or two of water in it and wipe the water away using a kitchen towel.

Pour ¼ cup batter into the centre of the pan. Spread and swirl the batter using the back of a ladle to make a thin circular shape about 7–8 inches in diameter. Increase the heat to medium and drizzle a tsp oil along the edges of the moong-lette. Cook until it is golden from the bottom, about 2–3 minutes. Flip and cook on the other side, about 1 minute.

Fold in thirds (see photo) and set aside. Repeat with the rest of the mixture, splashing the pan with water in between.

Serve on a plate with Scraptastic Orange Peel Chutney (page 121) and Roasted Peanut Chutney (page 115).

Good Mood Oatcakes

V / PF
35 minutes + resting time
Makes 8 oatcakes

GATHER

1 cup medium rolled oats
1 cup steel-cut oats
1 cup whole wheat flour
1 Tbsp brown sugar
1 tsp salt
½ tsp baking soda
¼ cup ghee (or ½ cup butter, softened)
¼ cup hot water

Equipment
Blender; mixing bowl; pastry cutter

HOW TO EAT

Serve with salad or as a dipper with soups and stews.

This recipe came about in those very early days of the pandemic when we were all in quarantine with limited access to fresh ingredients. It was also the time when my family was eating in front of the TV every night. Made entirely out of pantry ingredients, these oatcakes added fun back into our everyday mundane routine. Savoury, crumbly, occasionally chewy, they go well with a lot of dishes. But while they shine with many foods, they are truly exceptional as dippers for stews and soups, especially India-Style No-Cream of Tomato Soup (page 185).

PSA per my kids, who insisted I add this in: oatcakes are not actual "cakes." (Recipe pictured on page 184.)

MAKE

Mix the 2 types of oats together and blitz in a blender until the mixture is blended but still coarse. Pour the mixture into a large mixing bowl. Add the flour, sugar, salt, baking soda, and ghee and mix with a pastry cutter. Knead the mixture together with your hands to form a chunky ball.

Slowly add the hot water 1 Tbsp at a time, allowing enough time for the liquid to absorb into the oat and flour mixture. Knead to bring the dough together and form the mixture into a rough log.

Chill in the refrigerator for 30 minutes. Preheat the oven to 375°F.

Line a baking pan with a silicone mat and roll the log onto it. Cut the log into ¼-inch-thick slices and bake for 20 minutes, flipping halfway, at 10 minutes.

You can also cook the oatcakes on the stovetop: Heat a stainless steel skillet on medium-high. Once it is hot, turn the heat down to medium-low and lay the dough slices in the pan, without overcrowding. Cook on one side for about 7 minutes, then flip and cook on the other side, approx. 5 minutes.

Cool completely and store in an airtight glass container for up to 2 weeks.

Chickpea Socca

Vg / PF
25 minutes + resting time
Makes 2 large socca

GATHER

2 cups chickpea flour

2 cups water

1 cup finely chopped cilantro

6 Tbsp olive oil (approx.)

1 Tbsp lime juice (approx. ½ lime)

2 tsp sea salt

1 tsp coriander powder

1 tsp sugar

½ tsp red chili flakes

¼ tsp black pepper

1 tsp finely chopped rosemary

1 cup cooked chickpeas or rinsed
    canned chickpeas

1 cup loosely packed greens (e.g.,
    arugula, beet tops, radish greens),
    chopped into thin ribbons

Handful of pine nuts (or crushed
    roasted peanuts)

Equipment

Heavy-bottomed, stainless steel
(oven-safe) skillet; mixing bowl

Chickpea flour is wildly popular in many different cuisines around the world. One of my favourite dishes made with this hearty, robust flour is a dish called *socca*, which I like to think of as the Italian cousin of the Indian *puda* (you can find that recipe on page 165). With some crucial differences. Where puda is a thin, crisp crepe made on the stove, socca is thicker, almost pillowy, and grilled in the oven. Both are amazing in their own way and have their place of honour in my kitchen. Making socca can be a little tricky and may take some testing (and tasting) to get the ratio of liquid to vegetables to chickpea flour just right, but trust me, it's totally worth it.

MAKE

In a large mixing bowl, stir together the chickpea flour and water. Add the cilantro, 2 Tbsp of the olive oil, the lime juice, salt, coriander powder, sugar, chili flakes, and black pepper. Whisk everything together to combine. The batter should be thick, almost resembling pancake batter. Cover and set aside for 30 minutes.

Preheat the broiler to high/450°F. Add 2 Tbsp of the olive oil to a large, oven-safe skillet and swirl it around to coat the sides of the pan too. Add half the rosemary, chickpeas, and greens to the pan. Place the pan in the oven about 6–8 inches away from the grill. Allow enough time to wilt the greens and get a slight char to the chickpeas, about 3 minutes.

Pour half the batter into the pan to make the first socca. Swirl the batter around to cover the greens and chickpeas. Broil until the socca is golden and crispy and starts to pull away from the edges, 4–5 minutes. Take the pan out and sprinkle half the pine nuts on top with a drizzle of olive oil. Return to the broiler and grill for 1 minute.

Slide the socca onto a clean plate; it should come off the pan easily. If not, put it back in the oven for another minute.

Repeat with the remaining olive oil, rosemary, chickpeas, greens, and batter.

HOW TO EAT

Serve with fresh greens and a dollop of thickened yogurt.

Cool and freeze what you don't plan to eat in a few days. Reheat in a skillet on the stove and add a drizzle of olive oil and some fresh rosemary just before eating.

VARIATIONS

Swap the chickpeas and rosemary for grated carrot, shredded cabbage, or zucchini.

Place sliced tomatoes on top of the batter and then grill.

#GOGREEN TIP

Use the grill time to heat or cook other dishes in the oven. Multitasking large appliances will take our energy use further—easy on the wallet and on the planet!

Scene-Stealing
Small Plates

Lebanese-Style Rice and Lentil Mujaddarah

V / FF
1 hour
Make 8–10 servings

GATHER

1 cup wheat berries, rinsed and drained

6 cups water (approx.)

1 tsp salt (approx.)

6 Tbsp olive oil

1 cup whole brown lentils, rinsed and drained

1½ tsp cumin powder

4 cups sliced onions

1 cup long-grain rice (e.g., basmati), rinsed and drained

1 Tbsp ghee

½ tsp black pepper

Chopped mint leaves, for garnish

Cumin powder, for garnish

Once upon a time, my husband and I were living our best lives in the bustling coastal city of Dubai. We were young, recently married, and footloose, years before the kids came. My job at British Airways helped us travel often, and far. One of the joys of Dubai is that it is a meeting ground for cultures and cuisines, and the food culture is truly exceptional. Take *mujaddarah*—also *mujadara* or *mujaddara*, pronounced *m'jaddara* in Arabic—a popular Lebanese-style dish that is made with cooked lentils and rice and then finished with fried onions. Packed with tons of flavour and good-for-the-gut ingredients, it may even transport you to the Middle East with that first bite.

MAKE

Add the wheat berries to a large, heavy-bottomed pot along with 3 cups of the water and a generous pinch of salt. Add 2 Tbsp of the olive oil and bring the mixture to a boil. Turn the heat down to a simmer and cook for 20 minutes. Check and stir at the 10-minute mark. Add another cup of water if the wheat berries are drying out and sticking to the bottom of the pot.

After 20 minutes, add the lentils along with 1 cup water. There should be enough liquid in the pot for the mixture to swish around comfortably. Stir in ¾ tsp of the cumin powder, another big pinch of salt, and another 2 Tbsp of olive oil. Let the pot come to a boil again and then simmer on low for 20 minutes.

While the grains are cooking, place a skillet on medium-high heat. Add the remaining 2 Tbsp olive oil and bring to a shimmer. Add the sliced onions, turn the heat down to medium, and sauté. Stir regularly to allow the onions to cook gently until caramelized.

Check on the wheat berries and lentil mixture. They should be just past al dente and almost done. Squish a grain or two between your thumb and fingertips. They are ready when the grains are just squishable. Add the rice, the remaining 2 cups water, the ghee, a big pinch of salt, the pepper, and the remaining ¾ tsp cumin powder to the pot, stir once, and leave the lid on to cook for another 15 minutes.

#GOGREEN TIP
Promote biodiversity and support your gut-health by swapping out wheat berries with an ancient grain like kamut or teff. Cook until tender.

The onions should be amber-golden and caramelized by now. Turn the heat off.

Once the rice is cooked and most of the water has been absorbed, check for salt and add more if needed. Add in the caramelized onions and stir gently. Scrape the grains away from the sides of the pan and mix, taking care not to break the rice grains. Place the lid back on. Turn the heat off and leave the pot undisturbed for 5–10 minutes.

Garnish with the mint leaves and cumin powder and serve warm along with a fresh salad. Tart flavours and cool yogurt go well with mujaddarah.

COOKING HACK

Having company over? Make the mujaddarah a day or two beforehand. Reheat in the microwave or on the stove top with 1 or 2 Tbsp of water.

Mellow Yellow Daal Tadka

V / PF
35 minutes
Makes 4–5 servings

GATHER

1 cup yellow pigeon pea lentils (check label for *arhar* or *toor daal*)

4 cups water

Thumbnail-sized piece of ginger

1 tsp turmeric

1 whole green chili (optional)

1/3 tsp salt (approx.) to taste

1 cup chopped zucchini or greens (optional)

½ tsp sugar

¼ tsp cumin powder

¼ tsp red chili powder

For the Tadka

3 Tbsp ghee

½ tsp cumin seeds

2 garlic cloves, thinly sliced

¼ cup finely chopped onions

¼ cup finely chopped tomato

Daal tadka is yellow daal cooked together with ginger and turmeric, then finished with a hot oil tadka of tomatoes and onions. It is truly *ghar ka khana*, homemade food cooked for the family, and so, of course, it is often taken for granted. Mellow and quite yellow, my version of this daal is simple at its core, yet every time I make it in front of an audience, it gets the reception of a rock star!

MAKE

Rinse the lentils in fresh water a few times and drain. Add them to a large, heavy-bottomed saucepan along with the water, ginger, turmeric, green chili (if using), and salt to taste. Bring to a boil and then turn down to simmer for 20 minutes. The texture of the cooked daal should be smushy, but the grains should still hold their shape.

Turn the heat off and add the chopped zucchini or greens (if using), sugar, cumin, and chili powder. Stir, taste, and adjust seasoning if needed. Place the lid back on while you get the tadka ready.

For the Tadka

Heat the ghee on high in a small pan. Turn the heat down to medium and add the cumin seeds and sliced garlic, then the onions and tomatoes, and cook together for 5 minutes. Once the mixture looks jammy in texture and yet crispy, pour it on top of the hot daal. Watch for the sizzle.

HOW TO EAT

Serve with chapatti (page 99) or cooked whole grain barley.

VARIATIONS

Swap out the zucchini for orange pumpkin, or the greens for snow pea tips.

Try a different yellow daal: skinless yellow moong lentils if you have less than 20 minutes, or yellow split peas if you have 40 minutes or more. Still mellow, still yellow, and quite delicious.

Rice and Yellow Lentil Khichdi

V / PF
30 minutes
Makes 4–6 servings

GATHER

1 cup dried yellow split lentils (moong daal)
1 cup basmati rice
5½ cups water (approx.)
1 tsp ghee
⅓ tsp turmeric powder
Thumbnail-sized piece of ginger
Salt to taste

For the Tadka
1 Tbsp ghee
½ tsp cumin seeds
½ tsp turmeric powder
Handful of curry leaves, dry or fresh

Khichdi, also spelled *kitchari,* is a comforting and nourishing dish made with rice and yellow split moong lentils. Its soothing and slightly soupy texture reminds me of cool days. Khichdi has been enjoyed in India for generations, and it seems as if every culture and community has its own version.

This is my version, inspired by my mom's recipe. She learned from her mom, who likely learned it from her own. Hopefully, the cycle continues unbroken.

MAKE

Rinse the lentils and rice together 4–5 times until the water runs clear. Add them to a heavy-bottomed saucepan on high heat, along with the water, ghee, turmeric, ginger, and salt. Let the mixture come to a boil and then cover with a lid, turn the heat way down to a low simmer, and cook for 25 minutes. This dish should have a stewy consistency; add more water while the khichdi is simmering, if the mixture looks dry.

For the Tadka
When the khichdi is almost cooked, heat the ghee in a small pan on medium. Add the cumin seeds and let them sputter, about 30 seconds. Add the turmeric powder and sauté for another 15 seconds. Crush the curry leaves between the palms of your hands and add them in. The leaves will sputter, so watch out. Sauté the leaves for 15–30 seconds and then pour this sputtering mixture on the khichdi just as you're sitting down to eat.

HOW TO EAT
With yogurt if possible. Traditional wisdom from India considers yogurt, rice, and lentils a powerful combination for gut health.

India-Style No-Cream
of Tomato Soup

Vg / PF / LW
35 minutes
Makes 4 servings

GATHER

3 Tbsp olive oil

1 Tbsp fennel seeds

2 bay leaves

4 cloves garlic, finely chopped

2 lbs (1 kg) tomatoes, washed and
    quartered

½ tsp brown sugar

1 tsp turmeric powder

½ tsp black pepper

½ tsp salt

3 cups hot water (approx.)

Equipment
Immersion blender

Everyone should learn how to make a basic vegetable soup—and then learn how to take it up a notch with different veggies and brighter, bolder flavours. This is my version of the classic tomato soup. Once you're comfortable with this technique, I encourage you to use it for other veggies too. Choose what's seasonal for you. I have made luscious and lovely versions with green and yellow squash, zucchini, cauliflower, and even cabbage.

MAKE

Add the olive oil to a heavy-bottomed, comfortably sized saucepan on medium heat and wait until the oil shimmers. Turn it down to medium-low and add the fennel seeds, bay leaves, and garlic, in that order. Sauté for 45 seconds.

It's time for the tomatoes. Add them and then the sugar, turmeric, black pepper, and salt. Toss the mixture a few times to coat the tomatoes with the oil, aromatics, and spices. Turn the heat up to medium-high, cover the saucepan, and allow the mixture to simmer for 7–8 minutes. This will help the tomatoes release their liquid. Turn the heat down to medium-low and let it all cook together for 10 minutes. Now add the water, a cup at a time. Less is better at this stage; you can always add more water when you're finishing the soup.

Take the bay leaves out and then blend the tomato mixture using an immersion blender. Add another cup of water if needed and put the pan back on simmer for a minute. Taste and adjust the seasoning as needed.

HOW TO EAT
Serve in bowls with a drizzle of olive oil and a sprinkle of red chili powder. Add croutons (page 143) and serve with Good Mood Oatcakes (page 170).

Any Greens Saag Paneer

V / LW
40 minutes
Makes 4 servings

GATHER

2 big bunches of greens (about 1 lb),
    washed and trimmed

½ cup water (approx.)

2 Tbsp ghee

1 tsp cumin seeds

2 bay leaves

½ cup finely diced red onions

1 green chili, sliced lengthwise

1 Tbsp finely chopped ginger

1½ Tbsp finely chopped garlic

7 oz (200 g) paneer, diced into 1-inch
    cubes

½ tsp Kashmiri red chili powder

½ tsp salt (approx.)

1 tsp lime juice

1 Tbsp cream

½ tsp My Mom's Garam Masala Blend
    (page 133)

1½ Tbsp thinly sliced (matchsticks)
    ginger

Equipment

Immersion blender

Saag is the Hindi word for cooked greens. Paneer is a fresh, non-melting, occasionally homemade cheese (see my recipe on page 95). Together with onions and spices, they make saag paneer, a dish with heaps of delicate flavour and incredible potential. The saag can be made with any kind of leafy vegetable; I often use a combination of sweet leafy greens like amaranth, sorrel, Swiss chard, and spinach. Bitter greens like collard and rapini also shine in this dish, but they may need a sprinkle or two of sugar to complement the paneer.

MAKE

Put the greens in a large pot, add ½ cup water, and turn the heat to medium-high. Cover with a lid and steam the greens for 5–7 minutes. Tougher greens like kale may take an extra minute compared with spinach. Once the leaves are soft and pliable, use an immersion blender to purée them into a smooth mixture. Add a very small amount of water, if needed.

Add the ghee to a skillet on medium heat. Next, add the cumin seeds and bay leaves and sputter for 1 minute. Add the onions, green chili, and ginger and sauté until the onions are translucent, about 3 minutes. Then add the garlic and cook for 2 minutes.

The paneer comes next. Add the cubes and sauté for 2 minutes. The onions should be lightly browned by now, and there should be light colour on the paneer cubes too. Add the puréed greens, chili powder, and salt. Cover and cook for 5–6 minutes. Drizzle in the lime juice right at the end.

Garnish with a drizzle of cream, a sprinkle of garam masala, and sliced ginger on top.

HOW TO EAT

Serve with chapatti (page 99) or a bowl of cooked grains such as millet, rice, or barley.

Cucumber Curry Salad
with a Peanut Tadka

Vg
15 minutes
Makes 4 small servings

GATHER

2 cups diced cucumbers

1 cup diced red or yellow bell peppers

1 Tbsp lime juice (approx. ½ lime)

¼ tsp salt

For the Tadka

2 tsp olive oil

1 tsp black mustard seeds

2 green chilies, chopped

½ tsp turmeric powder

½ cup cooked chickpeas (optional)

¼ cup coarsely chopped, blanched peanuts

1 tsp lime juice

Big pinch of sugar

Equipment

Mixing bowl

I used to believe salads were an excuse for people to eat lettuce, and since the lettuce crop needs excessive amounts of water and attention to grow, I was never a fan. The lettuce story is far worse than I imagined, though. Seventy-one percent of the lettuce eaten in the United States is grown in California, a state that is facing record-breaking drought conditions.[2] And then there's the waste; this wildly popular, resource-intensive vegetable, if not stored correctly, turns to slime pretty quickly. So, for a long time, I avoided lettuce and ate very few salads, until one day I made this crunchy lettuce-free salad with a golden peanut tadka.

MAKE

Toss the diced vegetables with the lime juice and salt, and set aside.

For the Tadka

Add the oil to a small saucepan on medium heat and let it shimmer. Add the mustard seeds and let them crackle for 30 seconds. Next, add the chopped green chilies, turmeric powder, and chickpeas (if using). Let it all sizzle together.

Mix in the chopped peanuts and lime juice and toss together for another minute. Lastly, add the sugar and toss. The tadka is ready. Pour it on the cucumber mixture just as you sit down to eat.

VARIATION

Swap the peanuts for sunflower seeds; they add a similar crunch.

Skillet-Roasted Veggies

V / LW
25 minutes
Makes 4 servings

GATHER

½ small head broccoli, with leaves and stems and all

½ small head cauliflower florets, with leaves and stems and all

1 cup broccolini florets, leave the stems on

2 Tbsp ghee

½ tsp cumin seeds

3 cloves garlic, thinly sliced

⅓ tsp salt (approx.)

⅓ tsp black pepper

Squeeze of lemon juice

½ tsp chili flakes or paprika (optional)

2 Tbsp sesame seeds (optional)

I say this with no exaggeration: This dish is, hands down, the most delicious way to eat your veggies regularly. And it comes together with no special tools or extra ingredients.

People often ask, "What's your secret to cooking veggies?" Here it is: heat on high, lightly char the veggies, use some fat, season well, and add a splash of water at the end but not too much. Broccoli, broccolini, cauliflower, and even the much-maligned Brussels sprout will retain most of their colour and nutritional value cooked in this way, and the technique allows the flavour of the vegetables to really shine.

MAKE

Rinse the broccoli and cauliflower. Cut into florets, keep the leaves and rinse again, and slice the stems into coins.

Heat the ghee in a medium-hot skillet. Add the cumin seeds and garlic to the pan and sauté for 2 minutes. Turn the heat to high, add the sliced stems, and toss for 1 minute. Move quickly because the pan is hot. The florets go next, along with the leaves. Toss lightly for a few minutes, until the florets get a light char. Add the salt, pepper, and lemon juice.

Here's the secret: Turn the heat to medium and add 1–2 Tbsp water. Cover the pan for 1 minute, no more. Remove the lid and toss everything together until the stems are cooked through. That's it.

When I have company coming, I add ½ tsp chili flakes to the ghee in the beginning and the sesame seeds at the end.

HOW TO EAT

Serve on top of cooked whole grains (see page 97) with a dollop of yogurt on the side.

The combination of probiotic-richness from yogurt and the prebiotic fibre from vegetables is a wonderful pairing to support gut-health.

#GOGREEN TIP
Wash the lemon before squeezing for the juice. Use the zest and sliced peels, too, for a bright citrusy flavour.

No-Waste Corn and Barley-sotto

V / PF / LW
2 hours soaking +
40 minutes cooking
Makes 4 servings

GATHER

3 Tbsp olive oil

¼ cup finely chopped onions

1 Tbsp chopped garlic

¼ cup chopped apples

1 cup unprocessed pot barley, rinsed
   and soaked in warm water for 2 hours

4 cups Scrappy Stock, made with
   corncobs (page 81)

1 cup dry white wine (leftover is best)

½ cup + 2 Tbsp fresh corn kernels

¼ cup grated aged white cheese like
   parmesan or pecorino

¼ tsp freshly ground black pepper

2 garlic cloves, sliced

Handful of basil leaves

COOKING HACK

Double batch Scrappy Stock with corn
cobs and husks. Strain and freeze what
you don't need to make this pantry-forward meal another day.

There's just something soothing about stirring a pan, slowly cooking grains, adding liquid over time to draw out flavour and texture. That's risotto for you. Traditionally it is made with ingredients that don't need to try very hard: butter and cheese. It's easy to get delicious flavour with these rich ingredients, right? In this recipe, though, I show how easy it is to bring deep flavour with planet-friendly, good-for-the-gut, hardy foods too. The stock is made with rescued corncobs and husks that infuse deep flavour into barley (a whole grain often reserved for animals and beer), finally topped with an olive oil tadka that truly brings this risotto together.

MAKE

Place a heavy-bottomed, deep skillet on medium heat and add 1 Tbsp of the olive oil. Add the onions and garlic and gently sauté for 1 minute. Add the chopped apples and allow enough time to cook through, about 3 minutes total.

Add the soaked barley and toss the grains to toast them in the olive oil mixture for 2–3 minutes.

In a separate saucepan, stir together the corn stock and the wine and heat to a low simmer. Set aside.

To the toasted barley, add a ½ cup of the stock-and-wine mixture and stir. Repeat every 5–6 minutes on medium-low heat, adding ½ cup and stirring each time. Halfway through, add ½ cup of the corn kernels and let them cook along with the barley. Continue adding liquid and stirring every 5 minutes. Repeat until the grains are cooked and the liquid mixture has been almost absorbed, about 30 minutes total. Add in the cheese and the black pepper and stir through. Taste and adjust the seasoning.

To finish: Make an olive oil tadka. Heat the remaining 2 Tbsp olive oil in a small saucepan on medium heat. Add the sliced garlic and remaining 2 Tbsp corn kernels to the pan and sauté for another minute. Use the tadka technique from the Mellow Yellow Daal Tadka recipe (page 181) to crisp up the garlic. Pour it on top just as you're sitting down to eat. Garnish with a handful of basil leaves.

Make-It-Your-Own Mains

Not So Old-Fashioned Creamed Greens

V / LW
25 minutes
Makes 4 servings

GATHER

3 Tbsp olive oil

3 garlic cloves, crushed

3 Tbsp chickpea flour

5 cups fresh greens, chopped into finger-width ribbons

3 cups milk (whole or 2%)

½ tsp salt (or to taste)

½ tsp black pepper

¼ tsp freshly grated nutmeg

VARIATION

For a dairy-free version, swap out the milk for a 14 oz (400 mL) can of coconut milk. Dilute with 1 cup of water if needed.

COOKING HACK:

Cream a big batch of greens on Sunday afternoon so you can enjoy the vegetables all week long.

The technique of creaming adds flavour and creaminess to what people often consider boring food. I switch the technique and ingredients up a little in my version of this dish. Instead of all-purpose flour, I use chickpea flour. For the greens, I use whatever kind of leafy vegetable is in season: rapini, Swiss chard, collard, squash leaves, kale, or perhaps something else that is wilting in the back of the fridge. I like this dish saucy, so reduce the milk if you like it a little less so.

MAKE

Heat a deep saucepan on medium-high and add the olive oil. Add the crushed garlic and stir it in the oil until the garlic is partially cooked through, 45 seconds.

Turn the heat down to medium, add the chickpea flour, and stir it around for 2 minutes to gently roast. The flour will foam a little just at the start.

Add the greens and toss to coat them, then stir in the milk, salt, pepper, and nutmeg. Let the mixture come to a boil, and then turn it down to a medium simmer. Cook for 5 minutes until the milk thickens and the greens soften and look creamy.

#GOGREEN TIP
If using woodsy greens like kale and rapini, slice out the hardier stem parts and reserve them for Scrappy Stock (page 81).

Squash and Lentil Curry (Kaddu Ki Sabzi)

V / PF
40 minutes
Makes 6 servings

GATHER

2 Tbsp ghee
1 tsp black mustard seeds
⅓ tsp fenugreek seeds
2 Tbsp chopped ginger
Handful of curry leaves
1 cup whole French green lentils, rinsed
   and drained
1½ cups water (approx.)
1 cup thinly sliced red onions
2 cups diced (1 inch) acorn squash
   (or other hard variety of squash)
1 tsp coriander powder
½ tsp amchoor (or 1 Tbsp lime juice)
½ tsp red chili powder
½ tsp cumin powder
1 Tbsp brown sugar
Salt to taste

For the Tadka
1 Tbsp oil
1 Tbsp squash seeds
Handful of curry leaves
2 dried red or fresh green chilies, whole
   (optional)

For as long as I can remember, this sweet and sour Indian-style *kaddu ki sabzi* has been a weekly staple in my mom's kitchen. When I moved to Canada, I missed the flavours a lot and tried to re-create them with what was available locally. I remember testing a few combinations with lentils and various squash. This is where I finally ended up: a totally addictive, wholesome, and still accessible acorn squash and green lentil curry.

MAKE

Add the ghee to a heavy-bottomed pot on medium heat. Add the mustard and fenugreek seeds, ginger, and curry leaves, then the green lentils along with 1 cup water. Bring to a boil and then cover with a lid and turn down to simmer for 10 minutes.

Check the lentils; they should be pliable and half-cooked by now. Add the onions, ½ cup water, the squash, all the powdered spices, the sugar, and salt to taste. Cover and cook on low heat for 20 minutes. If the curry is sticking to the bottom of the pan, stir in another ½ cup water. The squash is cooked when it is soft when pushed gently with a spoon. Another sign that the kaddu curry is cooked is when you see some of the oil pool on the outer edges. Turn the heat off before the veggies and lentils start to mash together. Taste and adjust the spices, sugar, and amchoor to suit your palate. It should be a good balance of spicy, sweet, and sour.

For the Tadka
While the squash and lentils are cooking, heat the oil in a small, heavy-bottomed saucepan. Add the squash seeds, curry leaves, and whole chilies (if using). Let them sputter and cook for 30 seconds. Pour the sizzling hot tadka on the curry just as you are sitting down to eat.

HOW TO EAT
With chapatti or rice, and a bowl of yogurt.

COOKING HACK
Squash tough to peel? Slice it in half with a sharp knife and scoop out the fibrous guts and seeds. Drizzle 1 tsp oil in each half and add a sprinkle of turmeric powder. Microwave on high for 6 minutes. Let it cool, and then peel and chop.

#GOGREEN TIP
Some varieties of squash, such as delicata and acorn, can be cooked and eaten with their skin on—no waste.

Black-Eyed Peas (Raungi) Curry

V / PF
50 minutes
Makes 4–6 servings

GATHER

1 Tbsp ghee

½ tsp cumin seeds

2 black cardamom pods

1 bay leaf

4 garlic cloves, chopped

1 Tbsp chopped ginger

½ cup chopped red onions

⅔ cup passata tomato sauce (or another uncooked tomato sauce)

1 tsp coriander powder

½ tsp cumin powder

½ tsp turmeric powder

½ tsp garam masala

1 cup black-eyed peas (raungi), rinsed and drained

3 cups water (approx.)

⅓ tsp salt

Equipment

Instant Pot

Black-eyed peas, or *raungi*, are widely eaten in many parts of Asia and Africa. They are small, pale, oval-shaped beans with a black spot on one side, hence their name. Once cooked, they are creamy in texture, mild, and—I may be a little biased here—delicious. This dish is one of my favourite in this book, and while it may seem like it takes a while to cook, these beans are actually easier and faster to cook than many other varieties. And the time? It's mostly hands-free: you can close the lid and walk away.

MAKE

Turn the Instant Pot to sauté mode and add the ghee, then the cumin seeds, cardamom pods, and bay leaf. Sauté until the whole spices lightly brown and change aroma, about 30 seconds. Add the garlic and ginger and sauté for 1 minute.

Add the onions and sauté until they change colour, about 3 minutes. Once the onions have turned translucent, add the tomato sauce, coriander, cumin, turmeric, and garam masala. Sauté for another 3 minutes, stirring occasionally. Add the black-eyed peas, water, and salt.

Set the Instant Pot to 30 minutes on high pressure. Close the lid and walk away. Once the clock has run out, allow the steam to escape for 5 minutes so the Instant Pot is safe to open.

Open the lid, stir, and check for consistency—it should be soupy, so add 1 cup hot water if needed. Turn the Instant Pot to sauté mode and simmer for 5 minutes. Use the back of a ladle to mash a few of the beans. Taste and adjust the seasoning.

HOW TO EAT

Serve with rice and a bowl of yogurt.

COOKING HACK

Running short of time? Canned black-eyed peas work well in this dish. Use one 14 oz (398 mL) can; rinse and drain the beans and then follow the steps in the recipe, setting the Instant Pot to 10 minutes instead of 30.

Delhi-Style Chickpea Curry (Chana Masala)

V / PF
35 minutes
Makes 4 servings

GATHER

1 Tbsp ghee

1 tsp cumin seeds

1 bay leaf

2 black cardamom pods

2 tsp coriander powder

1 onion, chopped

4 garlic cloves, chopped

2 green chilies

2-inch piece ginger, finely chopped

Two 14 oz (398 mL) cans chickpeas, including the liquid

6 dates, pitted and chopped

1 Tbsp Deeply Sour and Sweet Tamarind Sauce (page 123) (or 1 Tbsp lime juice)

1 tea bag of plain black tea

4 cups water

1 tsp cumin powder

1 tsp smoked paprika

½ tsp amchoor

Chickpeas, or garbanzo beans as they are more commonly known in North America, are a delightful legume in so many ways. This spicy, tangy chana masala is a great example of this bean's versatility and how well it absorbs delicious flavours. What you end up with is a deeply nutritious, gorgeous dish that is made entirely using ingredients from the pantry.

MAKE

Place a large, heavy-bottomed pot or Dutch oven on medium heat and add the ghee, then the cumin seeds, bay leaf, and black cardamom. Allow the whole spices to sputter and change colour, about 1 minute.

Add the coriander powder and stir, allowing time for the powder to brown until almost charred, about 3–4 minutes. This is an important step to get the colour and deep flavour that is so unique to Delhi-style Chana Masala.

Once the coriander powder has been charred, add the onions, garlic, whole green chillies, and ginger. Stir and cook together until the aroma changes and the onions look translucent, about 3 minutes. Add the canned chickpeas (including the liquid) and dates to the pot, along with the tamarind sauce, tea bag, and water. (The tea bag lends the dark colour you see in the photo.)

Let this medley cook together on a steady simmer for 20 minutes. Then add the cumin powder, paprika, and amchoor and cook for 5 minutes. Use a potato masher or the back of a spoon to mash a few chickpeas together. This will bring the flavours of the curry together. Discard tea bag before serving.

RECIPE NOTE
Cooking dried chickpeas from scratch? Follow the Basic Way to Cook Beans (page 91) steps, add some of the cooking liquid, adjust the liquid and cooking time as needed, and then follow the recipe here.

HOW TO EAT
With chapatti (page 99) or whole grains (page 97).

Tangy Besan and Yogurt Kadhi

V
30 minutes
Makes 4 servings

GATHER

1 tsp ghee

½ tsp fenugreek seeds

1 tsp cumin seeds

½ tsp black mustard seeds

5 curry leaves

1 green chili, finely chopped, deseed if needed

¼ cup finely diced red onions

2½ cups water

2 cups plain yogurt

2 Tbsp chickpea flour (besan), mixed with 2 Tbsp water to form a slurry

1 tsp turmeric powder

1 tsp coriander powder

¼ tsp freshly ground black pepper

1 cup Besan and Broccoli Pakoras (page 153) (approx.)

For the Tadka

2 Tbsp grape-seed oil, or olive oil

Handful of curry leaves

3 dried red chilies

1 tsp cumin seeds

Finely chopped cilantro leaves to taste

Equipment

Kadhai

#GOGREEN TIP

Sour, days-old plain yogurt that's past its best-before date is best for this dish.

Kadhi, when said quickly, sounds similar to *curry*, but in reality, this dish is quite different from the curry you may be accustomed to. The flavours are tart and tangy, the preparation unfussy, and the presentation quite sumptuous. There's a version of this dish in almost every region in India. This one, paired with my Besan and Broccoli Pakoras (page 153), pays tribute to my Punjabi roots.

Kadhi is almost always finished with a hot oil tadka and served with rice on the side. I suggest eating it with other whole grains like millet to check all the Eating with Benefits boxes.

MAKE

Add the ghee to the kadhai and turn the heat to medium. Add the fenugreek seeds, cumin seeds, black mustard seeds, curry leaves, green chili, and onions, in that order, and lightly sauté for 2 minutes.

Whisk the water and yogurt together and then add the chickpea flour slurry, turmeric, coriander, and black pepper. Whisk this mixture into the contents of the kadhai. Bring to a boil and then turn down to simmer for 5 minutes. Add the pakoras and simmer for another 5 minutes.

For the Tadka

Heat the oil on medium in a small saucepan and add the curry leaves and red chilies. Let them sputter for a minute. Add the cumin seeds and stir until the aroma and colour change. Pour this tadka on the simmering kadhi and garnish with chopped cilantro.

HOW TO EAT

Serve with cooked whole grain millet on the side.

VARIATION

Skip the pakoras and instead use chopped veggies such as carrots sliced into 1-inch batons, frozen peas, and parboiled potatoes. Boil until the potatoes are cooked.

How to cook millet

Use hulled variety of millet (pale yellow in colour) for steaming. Rinse and soak the grains for 30 minutes while you cook your main dish. (Try it with the kadhi recipe on the previous page!) Rinse the grains again and place them in a saucepan. Add 2.5 parts water for every 1 part grains. Bring the mixture to a boil and then turn it down to a simmer. Cover with a lid and allow the mixture to cook for 20 minutes. The millet is cooked when steam tunnels form and the water has been absorbed. Fluff with a fork and serve.

#GOGREEN TIP

Millet is an ancient, drought-tolerant grain that has received very little attention over the decades. It's rich in fibre and protein, naturally gluten-free, and, when cooked well, has tons of flavour. While in India and Africa you can find many different types of millet, in North America it's usually the hulled versions of fox tail and pearl variety. The latter are small, yellow grains that can be cooked in as little time as rice.

Keema Aloo Shepherd's Pie

FF / HM
1 hour
Makes 6 servings

GATHER

4 Tbsp olive oil

1 tsp cumin seeds

2 black cardamom pods

1 tsp fennel seeds

6 garlic cloves, finely chopped

¼ cup finely chopped red onions

7 oz (200 g) ground chicken

14 oz (400 mL) can black or red beans,
    drained and rinsed

2 cups water

1 cup finely ribboned dark green leafy
    vegetables (or frozen peas)

1 cup passata tomato sauce (or another
    uncooked tomato purée)

Salt and pepper to taste

2 medium potatoes, boiled and peeled

1 large yam, boiled and peeled

2 Tbsp butter

¼ cup grated hard cheese, e.g.,
    Parmesan or pecorino (optional)

For the Tadka

2 Tbsp olive oil

2 Tbsp steel-cut oats

1 Tbsp chopped garlic

1 Tbsp finely chopped green onions

½ tsp mild to medium chili powder

Equipment

2 medium-sized stainless steel skillets

This dish is not as quick to make as most of the other dishes in this book, but once you get the hang of the ingredients and the practice of swapping out half the meat, you'll see that it comes together seamlessly.

The name is a fusion; *keema* is traditional stew-like curry made with ground meat and potatoes. That's the main layer in this shepherd's pie, a mix of ground chicken, beans, veggies, and various spices. The top layer is *aloo*, a potato and yam mash. The dish is finished with a crispy oat and garlic tadka. Like many Indian meat and bean dishes, this dish is freezer and fridge friendly; in fact, it tastes better after it has sat for a day in the fridge. Family friendly and company impressing, all at the same time.

MAKE

Heat the stainless steel skillet to high, and then add the olive oil. Turn the heat down to medium and add the cumin seeds, cardamom pods, and fennel seeds, in that order. Sauté for 1 minute in total. Once the seeds have turned a gentle brown and the aroma has changed, add the garlic and onions to the pan. Sauté until the onions are pale and translucent.

Now add the ground chicken, beans, water, veggies, tomato sauce, and salt and pepper. Scrape the bottom of the pan, stir everything together, and cover with a lid. Let the keema come to a boil, then turn down to simmer for 30 minutes.

Preheat the oven to 300°F.

While the keema is cooking, mash the potatoes and yam, along with the butter and salt and pepper to taste, until smooth.

Check on the keema. Stir it a couple of times and keep simmering until you see some of the oil pool on top of the meat and most of the water has cooked away.

It's time to assemble the keema aloo shepherd's pie. First, place an oven-safe skillet on medium-high heat, add a drizzle of oil, and swirl it around for 30 seconds. Turn the heat off. Layer in the keema mixture and smooth it out with the back of a spoon. Layer

Make-It-Your-Own Mains 207

the potato mixture on top and smooth it out. Add the cheese (if using) evenly over the top.

Freezer-friendly instructions: Double batch the ingredients and make two pies instead of one. Freeze one for up to 6 months. When you're ready to eat, thaw overnight and continue the steps for baking.

Place the skillet in the oven and bake for 15 minutes. Turn to broil at 450°F for the last minute. The dish is done when there's a slight browning on top of the aloo mixture. Remove the skillet from the oven.

For the Tadka

In a small, heavy-bottomed saucepan, heat the olive oil on medium-high and add the oats. Stir them around until lightly browned, about 2 minutes. Add the garlic and stir for another 2 minutes. Add the green onions, stir quickly and turn the heat off. Finally add in the red chili pepper powder and stir. Pour the sizzling tadka over the shepherd's pie. Let it sit for 5 minutes before serving.

HOW TO EAT

Enjoy with your favourite salad, cooked whole grains, or sliced baguette.

No-Waste Watermelon Rind Curry

Vg / PF / LW
30 Minutes
Makes 4 servings

GATHER

½ mini watermelon (approx.; enough
  for 2 cups sliced rind)
2 Tbsp olive oil
1 tsp black mustard seeds
⅔ tsp turmeric powder (or a generous
  thumbnail size amount of chopped
  fresh turmeric)
2 tsp finely chopped ginger
1 tsp sliced fresh red chilies (optional)
1 cup coconut milk
1 cup water
1 tsp lime juice
½ tsp salt (or to taste)
Lime wedges
Chopped cilantro
Crushed roasted peanuts

Mellow and aromatic, this watermelon rind curry is comfort food in a bowl. Every summer, we eat a lot of watermelons and the rinds normally end up discarded. Not with this dish! The rinds are the star here, for they add delicate flavour and texture to this soothing hug of a bowl. Prepping and cooking the rinds is not complicated either, and they absorb big flavours like ginger and turmeric well. The result is this enticing, delicious, good-for-you, good-for-the-planet curry.

MAKE

To prepare the watermelon rind: Wash the fruit very well. Slice it into manageable pieces and take the pink juicy part out to enjoy. Now, peel the outer green skin away and slice the white rind and remnants of the pink fruit into 2-inch-long batons.

Place a medium-sized skillet on the stove and turn the heat to medium. Add the oil. Once it is hot, add the mustard seeds. Allow the seeds to sputter, then add the turmeric, ginger, and chilies (if using). Toss and sauté until the ginger and turmeric have gently browned, a couple of minutes.

Add the watermelon rinds and toss them in the mixture for 1 minute. Add the coconut milk, water, lime juice, and salt and let it all simmer together for 20 minutes.

Garnish with the lime wedges, cilantro, and peanuts. Enjoy as a soup or with cooked millet or rice on the side.

VARIATION
Add tofu to make this a heartier meal. Slice the tofu into 1-inch-long rectangles and add it with the coconut milk. Let it all simmer together.

COOKING HACK
No crushed peanuts? Use sunflower seeds instead. Pan-roast gently in a skillet for a couple of minutes, cool and then crush using a rolling pin.

Kerala-Style Coconut Milk Curry

Vg / PF
30 minutes
Makes 4 servings

GATHER

4 green cardamom pods
Two 2-inch cinnamon sticks
⅓ tsp whole cloves
3 Tbsp coconut oil
2 Tbsp finely chopped ginger
2 green chilies, seeded and sliced
  lengthwise
1 medium onion, finely sliced
1 cup diced potatoes (bite-sized cubes)
½ cup chopped carrots (2-inch pieces)
2 cups cut green beans (2-inch pieces)
1 cup rinsed, diced tofu (1-inch cubes)
6 pearl onions (or 1 small red onion,
  cut into wedges)
14 oz (400 mL) can organic coconut
  milk
2 cups water
1 Tbsp lime juice (approx. ½ lime)
½ tsp freshly ground black pepper
Salt to taste

For the Tadka
2 tsp coconut oil

Equipment
Mortar and pestle; kadhai

VARIATIONS

Swap out the tofu for canned chickpeas
or another legume to make this meal even
more pantry friendly.

Swap out the potatoes for yams or sunchokes to add diversity to the plate.

If you search for Kerala coconut curry on the internet, you'll often see it described as a "stew" (pronounced *ishtew*), and that may be confusing because this dish is nothing like the stews you might be used to. This dish also does not resemble the popular Thai-style coconut milk curry that many of us enjoy. Instead, it is soft and harmonious in a way that is unique to the southern Indian state of Kerala. Its soothing nature is due to the use of whole spices like cardamom, cloves, black pepper, and cinnamon, which are indigenous to southern India. All of this truly makes for a one-of-a-kind curry.

MAKE

With a mortar and pestle, gently crush the whole cardamom, cinnamon, and cloves just enough to intensify their aroma. Fish the cardamom husks out and then crush the mixture another couple of times.

In a hot kadhai, on medium-high heat, add 3 Tbsp coconut oil and allow it to foam. Turn the heat to medium and add the crushed whole spice mixture. Give it 30 seconds and then add the ginger and green chilies and sauté for 2 minutes. Turn the heat down if the spices are browning too quickly.

Next, add the sliced onions and sauté for 3 minutes. Add the potatoes and toss for a minute. The carrots go next, then the beans, tofu, and pearl onions. Sauté together for 2 minutes. Stir in the coconut milk, water, and lime juice. Allow the curry to bubble on medium heat until the potatoes and carrots soften, about 15 minutes. Sprinkle in the freshly ground black pepper and salt. Taste and adjust the seasoning.

For the Tadka
In a small saucepan, heat 2 tsp coconut oil on medium. Once it's foaming, pour it on top of the curry to intensify the coconut flavour.

HOW TO EAT
With whole grains like plain steamed rice or millet on the side.

Good Mood Bolognese Sauce

PF | HM
50 minutes
Makes 6 servings

GATHER

1 cup French green lentils
1 Tbsp olive oil
1 tsp fennel seeds
2–3 bay leaves
6 cloves garlic, roughly chopped
1 cup chopped onions
10 oz (300 g) ground turkey
2 cups passata tomato sauce (or another uncooked tomato sauce)
1 cup chopped hardy vegetables (e.g., carrots, turnips, kohlrabi)
1 cup water (approx.)
1 Tbsp maple syrup
2 tsp turmeric powder
½ tsp red chili powder
Salt and black pepper to taste
2 Tbsp balsamic vinegar
Handful of chopped basil
Drizzle of olive oil

The first time I made this sauce I was stunned by how easily it came together. Contrary to what some may think, swapping out half the meat, turkey in this case, for lentils didn't take away any of the flavour; instead, it made this traditional sauce healthy and planet-friendly. Since that first time, I have made this Indian-spiced Italian sauce many times and have even cooked it on TV and at cooking workshops. Each time, I tweak it with what I have in my pantry, a new type of legume or spices depending on the season.

I hope you do the same and fall in love with this dish too.

MAKE

Rinse the lentils and let them soak while you get everything else ready.

Add the oil to a pot and turn the heat to medium. Add the fennel seeds and bay leaves and sauté for 1 minute. Once the seeds have turned a gentle brown and the aroma has changed, add the garlic and onions. Sauté until the onions are pale and translucent.

Add the rinsed lentils, ground turkey, tomato sauce, vegetables, water, maple syrup, turmeric, chili powder, and salt and pepper. Scrape the sides and the bottom of the pot, stir everything together, and cover with a lid. Let the mixture come to a boil, then turn the heat to medium-low and simmer for 30–45 minutes.

Check on the sauce occasionally and stir and scrape the bottom if needed. Add more water if it looks like it's drying up. The final consistency should be saucy. The bolognese is done when there is a sheen of oil on the surface. Lastly, stir in the balsamic vinegar and turn the heat off.

Garnish with a handful of chopped basil and a drizzle of olive oil.

HOW TO EAT
With pasta, whole grains, or a green salad on the side.

Railway Beef Curry

PF / HM
1 hour
Makes 6 servings

GATHER

2 tsp coriander powder

2 tsp turmeric powder

2 tsp paprika (or a spicier chili powder)

1 tsp cumin powder

1 tsp salt

10 oz (300 g) stewing beef

3 black cardamom pods

2 Tbsp coriander seeds

2 tsp cumin seeds

1 tsp fennel seeds

1 tsp black peppercorns

5 Tbsp ghee

6 small potatoes, skin on, halved

2 small red or green fresh chilies

3 bay leaves

Three 1-inch cinnamon sticks, lightly crushed

8 garlic cloves, finely chopped

2 Tbsp chopped ginger

2 cups finely sliced red onions

2 cups passata tomato sauce

2 cups water

A generous pinch of My Mom's Garam Masala Blend (page 133)

Cilantro leaves to taste

Equipment
Mortar and pestle; spice grinder; Instant Pot

While writing this cookbook, I made a deliberate choice to feature only one red meat dish. This one! The science community is in agreement: we need to move away from meat in our diet, and quickly, to slow down the worst effects of climate change around the world (see "Move Away from Meat," page 39). However, cutting out meat completely can be challenging; so what can we do instead? Eat less meat, way less, and when you do, cook a dish that tastes special and fantastic, like this Railway Beef Curry.

MAKE

Combine the coriander, turmeric, paprika, cumin, and salt in a bowl and toss the beef pieces with this dry marinade. Set aside.

With a mortar and pestle, crush the cardamom pods until the oil starts to ooze out. Set aside.

In a pan on low to medium heat, dry-roast the coriander seeds, cumin seeds, fennel seeds, and black peppercorns for 2 minutes. Crush them to a fine powder in the spice grinder and set aside.

Add 1 Tbsp of the ghee to a skillet on medium-high heat and fry the potato halves until golden, about 2 minutes. Set aside.

Turn the Instant Pot to sauté mode and add 3 Tbsp of the ghee. Toss in the fresh chilies and allow them to flavour the ghee. Take them out after 30 seconds if you are trying to hold back on the heat.

Add the crushed black cardamom pods, bay leaves, and cinnamon, and let them sizzle for a couple of minutes. Next, add the garlic and ginger and sauté until the mixture is a pale brown colour. Add the sliced onions and sauté on medium heat until they have turned golden, 6–7 minutes.

Stir in the tomato sauce and the dry-roasted spice mix you set aside earlier. Cook on medium heat for another few minutes until the oil leaves the sides of the inner pot, about 10 minutes in total. Add the beef pieces and fry until there is a thin layer of oil on top of the pieces and a gentle caramelization is visible, another 5 minutes.

Now add the fried potatoes and water. Place the lid on the Instant Pot and cook on high pressure for 20 minutes. Do a natural pressure release for 10 minutes.

Cooking on the stovetop? Place the lid on the pot and cook until the meat is fork-tender and can fall apart, 45 minutes–1 hour. Stir occasionally to avoid sticking and burning at the bottom.

Open the lid and add the remaining 1 Tbsp ghee and a generous pinch of garam masala. Stir together with a ladle. Garnish with the cilantro leaves on top and serve hot.

HOW TO EAT
Serve with yogurt and chapatti (page 99), or with rice or barley pulao.

#GOGREEN TIP
Ask your butcher for their least popular cuts of meat, for example bone-in shanks. They are often priced cheaper per unit, and because there is less demand for them, there is a risk they will end up in the landfill. Cook until you reach a fall-apart tender texture.

No-Waste Orange and Green Stir-Fry

GATHER

2 tsp olive oil

⅓ cup cashews

1 cup sliced onions

1 Tbsp chopped ginger

2 tsp chopped garlic

2 small fresh chilies, finely chopped

2 Tbsp finely chopped cilantro stems

2 Tbsp finely sliced orange peels

1 Tbsp organic miso paste

Zest of 1 lime

1 tsp coriander powder

½ tsp black pepper

2 Tbsp honey

8 oz (200 g) boneless, skinless chicken thighs, sliced into 2-inch strips

1 cup king oyster mushrooms, hard ends trimmed, sliced lengthwise

2 Tbsp sesame seeds

1 Tbsp lime juice (from the zested lime)

Salt to taste

2 cups broccolini with stems intact, washed

Handful of chopped cilantro leaves

I travel around the world regularly, often without leaving my kitchen. My roots are in India and our life today is in Canada, but my memories and experiences often take me past the shores of either country. This stir-fry, for example, brings the flavours of East and South Asia together with the spirit of Eating with Benefits. Supplementing the chicken with oyster mushrooms, as I have done here, makes this dish even more climate-smart (and adds incredible flavour and texture).

Use the orange peel sauce that you make in this recipe in other dishes too. It's versatile enough to complement tofu or paneer and a ton of different veggies.

MAKE

First, wash and prep all ingredients, stems and peels and all.

Add the oil to a heavy-bottomed pan, turn the heat to medium-high, and wait for the oil to shimmer. Turn the heat down to medium and roast the cashews for 1 minute. Remove them from the pan and set them aside.

Add the onions, ginger, and garlic, in that order, to the pan and cook for 5–6 minutes, stirring often. Add the chilies, cilantro stems, orange peels, miso paste, and lime zest. Loosen everything and break up the miso paste and toss and cook together for 2 minutes. Stir in the coriander powder, black pepper, and honey. Next, add the chicken and mushrooms and mix well with the sauce. Add the sesame seeds, lime juice, and salt, then toss and sauté until the chicken is cooked through, 10 minutes.

Add the broccolini and caramelize it with the chicken, about 5 minutes. Once you see a slight char on the veggies and the chicken is cooked, turn the heat off. Garnish with the roasted cashews and chopped cilantro sprinkled on top.

HOW TO EAT

Serve with steamed rice or other cooked whole grains (for ideas, see page 97).

VARIATIONS

Swap the broccolini for snap peas or green leafy vegetables. For crisp vegetables, add them at the end to avoid overcooking.

#GOGREEN TIP

Make this dish vegan by swapping all the meat with king oyster mushrooms. One of my favourite fungi, these mushrooms have a chewy, hearty texture that mimics chicken without the need for faux ingredients.

White Bean Turkey Chili

GATHER

1 Tbsp olive oil

1 tsp fennel seeds

2 black cardamom pods

2 bay leaves

8 garlic cloves, finely chopped

1 cup chopped white onions

10 oz (300 g) ground turkey

1 Tbsp coriander powder

½ tsp black pepper

19 oz (540 mL) can white or navy beans, drained and rinsed

1 cup sweet apple cider

Salt to taste

3 cups dark leafy greens

Lime juice and wedges

Chopped cilantro to taste

This dish came from my desire to experiment in the kitchen. You see, my kids loved traditional chili, the red and meaty kind, and in trying to make it at home I tested various combinations: swapping out red beans for white for a different colour palette; replacing beef with turkey for sustainable, healthy meat; and using new (to me) vegetables to make this dish wholesome.

Who knew then that trying something new would be good for our health and also support a diverse food system? Years later, this practice formed a cornerstone of the Eating with Benefits framework (see "Diversify Your Diet," page 36).

MAKE

Heat the oil in a heavy-bottomed pot on medium heat. Once you see the oil shimmer, add the fennel seeds, cardamom pods, and bay leaves. Toss and let the seeds brown gently, about 1 minute. Add the garlic and let it sauté for a couple of minutes.

Add the onions and cook on medium heat for 5 minutes. The onions will slowly turn translucent and release their liquid. Once that happens, add the ground turkey, coriander, and black pepper. Turn the heat to medium-high and allow the meat to brown for 4–5 minutes.

Add the beans and apple cider and cook on high for 1 minute. Turn the heat down to medium, add salt to taste, and stir it all together. Cover the pot with a lid and simmer on medium-low heat for 20 minutes. Stir halfway through to check that it's all coming together, and add water if needed.

Turn the heat off and stir in the greens. Put the lid back on and let the chili sit for a few minutes. Taste and adjust the salt and consistency to your preference.

Garnish with a drizzle of olive oil, a squeeze of lime juice, chopped cilantro, and lime wedges.

HOW TO EAT

Enjoy with sliced baguette or multi-grain loaves.

RECIPE NOTE

Cooking beans from scratch? See page 91 for steps on how to do this. Replace the canned beans in the chili recipe with 2 cups cooked beans.

Deeply Green Shakshuka

V / LW
40 minutes
Makes 4 servings

GATHER

3 Tbsp olive oil

6 garlic cloves, crushed

1 cup sliced leeks

¼ tsp salt (approx.)

1 cup chopped tomatillos or raw green
   tomatoes (or the juice of 1 lime)

1 tsp cumin powder

1 tsp coriander powder

¼ tsp red chili powder or paprika

10 cups leafy greens (like chard, kale,
   amaranth, collard, beet tops, spinach,
   and sorrel), sliced ribbon thin

Sprinkle of sugar

1 cup chopped cilantro

6 eggs

Black pepper to taste

Sprinkle of crumbled feta cheese (or the
   paneer curds, page 95)

Sliced jalapenos to taste

For the Crispy Tadka

2 Tbsp olive oil

3 garlic cloves, sliced

½ tsp paprika

I use the word *favourite* a number of times throughout this book because that's what these recipes are, a selection of my most beloved dishes that bring together the spirit behind Eating with Benefits. This is one of my favourite egg dishes, a green shakshuka where instead of the more popular tomato base, I recommend using slow-simmered dark, leafy greens. This switch transforms this already luscious dish into an absolutely impressive version, ideal for a big family brunch or a small and sumptuous dinner.

MAKE

Heat a medium skillet on medium-high heat and add the olive oil. Add the crushed garlic, leeks, and ¼ tsp salt and cook for 5 minutes. Turn the heat down to medium if the garlic starts to darken too much. Add the tomatillos, cumin, coriander, and chili powder. Stir everything together occasionally and cook until the aroma deepens, 2–3 minutes.

Increase the heat back to medium-high and add the greens by the handful to allow them to wilt and cook through. Cover as needed. Add more salt to taste and a sprinkle of sugar. Turn the heat down to medium and stir often until the greens have wilted and turned a deep green. There should be some liquid in the pan from the greens. Cook until the liquid has almost completely evaporated, about 20 minutes.

Taste and adjust the salt and seasoning. The tomatillos should add a slightly acidic flavour. (If that flavour is not noticeable, add a bit of lime juice.) Now stir in the chopped cilantro.

Make 6 small wells in the greens and crack 1 egg into each well. Sprinkle each egg lightly with salt and pepper. Cover the dish and cook for 3–5 minutes over low heat. The eggs are done when the whites have set and the yolks are slightly runny. Keep cooking a little longer if you would like the yolks to solidify further.

For the Crispy Tadka

While the eggs are cooking, add the oil to a small frying pan set over medium-high heat. Once the oil is sizzling hot, add the sliced garlic and stir until lightly golden, about 1–2 minutes. Turn the heat off and add the paprika. Spoon the crispy tadka on the eggs.

Garnish with a sprinkle of crumbled feta and sliced jalapenos on top.

HOW TO EAT
Serve immediately with a warm pita to scoop the greens.

#GOGREEN TIP
Eggs make a delicious, protein-rich, and climate-smart dinner.

Calcutta-Style Kathi Rolls

V / LW
40 minutes
Makes 4 rolls

GATHER

For the Paneer Filling

2 Tbsp olive oil

2 tsp finely chopped garlic

½ tsp turmeric powder

1 cup drained and dried homemade
  paneer curds (page 95) or 9 oz (250 g)
  store-bought paneer, cut into 1 × 2-inch
  rectangles

1 tsp cumin powder

¼ tsp salt

¼ tsp red chili powder

For the Chapatti Rolls

4 eggs

1 Tbsp water

Salt to taste

1 Tbsp olive oil (approx.)

4 whole grain chapattis (page 99)
  or store-bought whole grain tortillas

For Assembly

Sliced fresh greens like arugula or
  watercress

Fresh Cilantro and Mint Chutney
  (page 114)

Quick-pickled onions (page 87)

Kathi rolls are a staple on the busy streets of Kolkata, where carts can be spotted crowding the side of the road with vendors frying eggs and chapattis in hyperdrive. Traditionally, these rolls are made with grilled meats like lamb or mutton. My friend makes a killer version of this dish with her amazing slow-cooked masala chicken. In my vegetarian version, I smush—a technical cooking term—chapattis or when time is tight, store-bought tortillas onto scrambled eggs, tuck in grilled paneer cubes along with chutney and pickled onions. A sparkle of flavours, I promise!

MAKE

For the Paneer Filling

Heat the olive oil in a skillet on medium-high heat. Add the garlic and cook for 45 seconds. Add the turmeric powder and stir. Add the homemade paneer curds, cumin, salt, and chili powder. Toss to coat. Turn the heat to medium low, cover the skillet, and let the paneer cook for 5 minutes, stirring occasionally. Uncover the skillet and continue to cook to allow any liquid to evaporate. (If you're using store-bought paneer, the method remains the same, but you may need to add 2–3 Tbsp water to allow the mixture to come together and coat the paneer.)

For the Chapatti Rolls

Crack the eggs into a mixing bowl, add the water and salt to taste, whisk, and set aside.

Place a skillet on the stove on medium heat. Drizzle oil in the pan and lightly fry each chapatti (alternatively, use store-bought whole grain tortillas) for 15 seconds on one side only, then set it aside. In total, you will use approximately 1 Tbsp oil for 4 chapattis.

Next, pour one-quarter of the whisked eggs into the pan and swirl it around. Place 1 chapatti on top of the egg mixture, browned side down. Swirl around and let the egg continue to cook.

Use a flat spatula to flip the chapatti and egg combination so that the egg side is up. Cook the chapatti for 15 seconds and then set it aside on a plate. Cover with another plate so that it stays warm. Repeat with the remaining whisked eggs and chapattis.

For Assembly

Time to assemble the kathi rolls. Lay everything out, including the cooked paneer, sliced greens, chutney, and pickled onions.

On each of the eggy chapattis, start by laying sliced greens, then top with a few pieces of paneer, a drizzle of chutney, and lots of pickled onions. Roll and tuck one end under the other.

Repeat with the rest of the chapattis and enjoy!

HOW TO EAT

Enjoy as is! These rolls make a great portable snack or meal for tiny hands or midday lunches or festive potlucks! All the condiments and flavours you need are already tucked inside.

Turkish-Style Eggs (Cilbir)

GATHER

For the Yogurt Sauce
2 cups plain yogurt, lightly whisked
3 garlic cloves, thinly grated
¼ cup finely chopped dill (approx.)
Salt and pepper to taste

For the Poached Eggs
1 Tbsp vinegar
8 eggs

For the Hot, Spiced Butter
8 Tbsp butter
1 Tbsp finely chopped orange bell
   peppers
½ tsp Aleppo chili flakes (or another
   mild variety)
½ tsp cayenne pepper (or another spicy
   chili pepper variety)

HOW TO EAT

Serve with sourdough bread or multi-grain pita for scooping and mopping. You'll need it.

COOKING HACK

Use homemade yogurt (page 84) for a boost of probiotic richness.

Double-batch the spiced butter. Refrigerate what's left and reheat in the microwave for a quick weekday breakfast.

Pronounced *chil-bur*, this dish is quite simply poached eggs on a garlicky yogurt sauce, drizzled with hot, spiced butter. It is often served with fermented sourdough bread or warm multi-grain pita. I remember being skeptical when I first tried this dish—eggs and yogurt, together? Who would have thought this unexpected (to me) yet uncomplicated combination would create an incredible burst of flavour?

MAKE

For the Yogurt Sauce
Stir the ingredients together, leaving some dill to use as a garnish later. Taste. The sauce should be bright, garlicky, salty, and tangy, all at once. Put the mixture in a small saucepan on low heat until warm, 5 minutes. ***Note:*** overheating will curdle the yogurt.

For the Poached Eggs
Fill a large saucepan about 3 inches deep with room-temperature water. Add the vinegar and bring the water to a rolling boil, then turn down the heat to medium-low, so only a few bubbles are visible on the water's surface.

Break the eggs 1 at a time into a small bowl or ramekin and gently tip each egg into the pot. You may need to work in batches to avoid overcrowding. Poach the eggs until the whites firm up but the yolk is still soft inside, 3 minutes. Use a slotted spoon to transfer the eggs to a plate.

For the Hot, Spiced Butter
Melt the butter in a small saucepan on medium heat until it starts to foam and turn golden, 1–2 minutes. Turn the heat to medium-low and add the bell peppers. Let them cook and soften for about 5 minutes. Add the chili flakes and cayenne pepper and stir until the colour is uniform. Turn the heat off quickly to avoid burning.

To serve, divide the warm yogurt among 4 bowls; you need just under ½ cup for each serving. Swirl the mixture around using the back of a spoon. Top each bowl with 2 poached eggs, side by side. Spoon about 2 Tbsp of hot, spiced butter on top and around the eggs, and garnish with chopped dill.

Street-Style Egg Masala Fry

GATHER

4 eggs, room temperature

5¼ cups water

1 Tbsp ghee

1 tsp black mustard seeds

Handful of fresh or dried curry leaves

2 small green chilies, slit lengthwise (optional), deseed if needed

1 Tbsp thinly sliced ginger (½-inch pieces)

3 garlic cloves, finely chopped

1 tsp roasted fennel seed powder

1 tsp Kashmiri red chili powder

1½ cups thinly sliced red onions

½ tsp salt (approx.)

1½ cups whole grape tomatoes (or diced tomatoes)

½ tsp amchoor

½ tsp black pepper

1 Tbsp olive oil

1 tsp turmeric powder

Eating with your fingers is quite common in many traditional cultures around the world. In India, it's an enjoyable way to really connect with what we are eating, and scooping with pieces of roti makes sure we get all the yummy bits of this spicy and almost jammy Street-Style Egg Masala Fry. Aromatic and flavourful, this dish is a joy to savour, with skillet-roasted boiled eggs, sliced onions, tomatoes, turmeric, and curry leaves.

MAKE

To boil the eggs: Place the eggs in a saucepan and cover with 5 cups of water. Cover the pot with a lid and put it on the stove on high heat. Bring the water to a rolling boil, about 1 minute. Wait until there is enough steam built up to make the lid rattle. Turn the heat off, leave the saucepan covered, and set it aside for 12 minutes.

While you're waiting for the eggs to finish up, place a large skillet on medium heat. Add the ghee and let it heat through, then add the mustard seeds, curry leaves, and green chilies (if using). Heat until the seeds crackle, about 15 seconds. Add the ginger, garlic, fennel seed powder, and ½ tsp of red chili powder, in that order. Cook until the aroma of garlic changes from raw, about 2 minutes. Add the sliced onions along with a big pinch of salt and sauté this masala mixture for 5 minutes. Add the tomatoes and cook for another 3 minutes.

Check in on the eggs. Discard the hot water and cover the eggs with tap water. When they're cool enough to handle, peel the eggs, dry them gently, and slice them in half lengthwise. Season them with a big pinch of the salt, the remaining ½ tsp of the red chili powder, and ¼ tsp of the amchoor, and set aside.

Check in on the onion and tomato masala mixture. Squish the tomatoes with the back of a ladle to allow the liquid to escape and sizzle, and toss. Add the remaining ¼ cup water and ⅓ tsp salt, and cook, stirring occasionally, until the tomatoes and onions come to a jammy texture, about 10 minutes. Sprinkle in the black pepper and remaining ¼ tsp amchoor. Check for salt and seasoning. Add more if needed. Toss.

#GOGREEN TIP

The technique here used to boil eggs uses energy efficiently with little waste.

Move the masala to the outer edges of the pan. Add the oil to the centre of the pan and heat through. Turn the heat to medium high, add the turmeric powder and allow it to darken, but don't let it burn. Use tongs to gently place the halved eggs, white side down, in the pan. Allow the whites of the egg to get crispy and brown from the outside, about 2 minutes. Flip the eggs over so the yolks get some char too.

Move the masala around the halved eggs. It will continue to cook and dry out while the eggs fry in the oil. The dish is ready when the onion and tomato masala is dry, the egg whites are crispy on the outside, and the yolks are charred.

HOW TO EAT
Serve hot with naan or chapatti.

#GOGREEN TIP
Conserve water! Use the cooled water from the boiled eggs to water your houseplants.

Thai-Style Coconut Milk Braised Fish

PF / FF / LW
40 minutes
Makes 6 servings

GATHER

Four 6 oz (170 g) fillets of sustainably
  sourced white fish (e.g., haddock or
  cod), skin on
½ lime
2 tsp coriander seeds
2 tsp fennel seeds

For the Green Paste

1 small onion (or 2 small shallots),
  cut into 2-inch chunks
4 makrut lime leaves
Stems of a handful of cilantro, roots
  trimmed, washed well
2-inch stalk lemon grass, finely chopped
2-inch piece galangal (or ginger), cut in
  chunks
2 green chilies (optional)

For the Curry

1 Tbsp coconut oil
1 small onion, finely sliced
2 makrut lime leaves, lightly chopped
1 tsp turmeric powder
1-inch stalk lemon grass, lightly crushed
  with the back of a knife
1 tsp finely chopped galangal (or ginger)
14 oz (400 mL) can coconut milk
½ tsp salt
½ tsp sugar
Chopped cilantro to taste

Equipment

Large, oven-friendly skillet; blender

As a food writer, I'm often tasked with experimenting with ingredients and tweaking proportions to find the perfect recipe. There are usually many edits and variations. Every now and then though, I make a dish that needs no improvement. That's what happened with this coconut milk braised fish. It was perfect the first time around. Since then, I have cooked this dish a dozen times, with many changes depending on what I have in the fridge, and each time, without fail, it is just exceptional.

MAKE

Rinse the fish and squeeze the juice of ½ a lime on the fillets. Set the fish aside, skin side up.

In a skillet on medium-high heat, roast the coriander and fennel seeds, tossing until they have browned gently and the aroma has warmed and changed, about 3 minutes. Set aside to cool.

For the Green Paste

Put all the ingredients for the green paste in a blender in the order they are listed. Blend until smooth, adding the roasted coriander and fennel seeds halfway through. Add a drizzle or two of olive oil, if needed, to bring the mixture together.

For the Curry

Place a large, oven-friendly skillet on high heat and add the coconut oil. Turn it down to medium, add the sliced onions, and toss. After 1 minute, add the chopped lime leaves, turmeric powder, crushed lemon grass, and chopped galangal. Toss and sauté for 2 minutes.

Add 2 Tbsp of the green paste blended earlier and sauté until the aroma changes from raw, about 5 minutes. Now stir in the coconut milk, salt, and sugar. Simmer for 15–18 minutes to allow the flavours of the green paste to infuse the coconut milk. Taste-test. The raw onions and cilantro stems should be cooked thoroughly by now. The sauce should taste extra salty because you're adding the fish next.

Place the fish in the green curry, skin side up, and simmer for 5 minutes. Fish cooks quickly, so stay vigilant to avoid overcooking. Spoon some of the sauce on top of the fish and place the skillet under a hot grill at 450°F for 3 minutes to caramelize the fish skin and allow it to get crispy. Garnish with the chopped cilantro.

HOW TO EAT
Serve with steamed rice and/or a green salad.

COOKING HACK
Green paste left over? It's freezer friendly and can be stored for up to 1 year. Thaw it overnight and use with tofu or chicken, or to make Thai-style Braised Fish another day.

Lime leaves

These aromatic leaves are often incorrectly compared to bay leaves. Unlike bay leaves, lime leaves have an incredibly fresh citrus flavour. Avoid referring to this herb as "kaffir lime," though; the word *kaffir* is an offensive term for many people. The fruit's actual name is makrut lime, or simply Thai lime.

Pan-Fried Golden Fish with Tahini and Caramelized Onions

30 minutes
Makes 4 servings

GATHER

Four 6 oz (170 g) fillets of sustainably caught robust white fish (e.g., cod or haddock)

½ lime

1 tsp coriander powder

½ tsp cumin powder

½ tsp turmeric powder

2 Tbsp pine nuts

4 Tbsp olive oil

1 large onion, thinly sliced

1 garlic clove, very finely chopped

⅓ cup tahini

Juice of ½ lime

Salt and pepper to taste

Sprinkle of sugar

¼ cup finely chopped mint leaves (optional)

COOKING HACK

Make a triple batch of the caramelized onions and save on energy/cooking costs. Use the remaining onions for the Lebanese-Style Rice and Lentil Mujaddarah (page 177).

#GOGREEN TIP

Find the most sustainable option for fish in your area. Or buy local, whatever local means to you. Check the resources at the back of the book for options.

This dish is different from what I typically make. Don't get me wrong; it's similar in that it uses few ingredients and simple steps, but it stands out because it was inspired by a meal I ate at a restaurant in Mumbai, India. Usually, my inspiration comes from home cooking but this time it was different. When I came back home to Toronto, I tried to re-create the flavours in various ways, but I failed because the unique flavours of locally caught fish from the Arabian Sea simply cannot be replicated, right? After much playing with fish and flavours and a few failed experiments, this dish, finally, comes pretty close!

MAKE

Rub the fish fillets with the lime and sprinkle them with the coriander, cumin, and turmeric. Allow the flavours to marinate for 15 minutes.

While the fish is marinating, place a small pan on medium heat and dry-roast the pine nuts for 1 minute. Set aside.

In a medium-hot skillet, heat 3 Tbsp of the olive oil. Add the sliced onions and sauté, stirring occasionally, until they're caramelized, about 15 minutes. Turn the heat down to low-medium a few minutes in to the cooking process to keep the onions from burning. Set aside.

Turn the heat to medium and, in the same pan, add the remaining 1 Tbsp olive oil and the garlic and swirl it around. Place the marinated fish in the pan and brown on one side for 2–3 minutes. Flip carefully and brown on the other side for about 2 minutes. Take the fish out and set it aside.

In the same pan, whisk together the tahini, lime juice, salt, pepper, and a pinch of sugar to taste. Heat through for 1 minute. Taste and adjust the seasoning. If needed, add ¼ cup water to make a pouring (but not runny) consistency. This sauce solidifies a little as it comes to room temperature. Whisk in the mint (if using). Set the sauce aside in a bowl.

Top the fish with the caramelized onions and toasted pine nuts, drizzle it with the tahini sauce, and serve immediately.

Not So Traditional Golden Fish Cakes

FF / PF
20 minutes
Makes 8 fish cakes

GATHER

7 oz (approx. 200 g) sustainably sourced canned salmon or tuna

½ cup instant oats

½ cup finely diced tomatoes

½ cup diced zucchini

½ cup finely chopped onions

2 tsp finely chopped garlic

1 tsp turmeric powder

1 tsp coriander powder

½ tsp cumin powder

3 Tbsp applesauce

2 Tbsp chickpea flour (approx.)

Salt to taste

2 Tbsp olive oil

Equipment
Mixing bowl; pastry cutter

My kids are obsessed with these fish cakes. They are on weekly rotation in our house, and with oats, turmeric, and a mix of veggies, these are healthy and easy to put together for a quick weeknight meal.

Canned fish is a pantry staple around the world. It's affordable, shelf stable, and can be found sustainably caught. The variety is great too: tuna, salmon, sardines, herring, and more. I make these fish cakes with either tuna or salmon. Eat as burgers or alongside whole grains or fresh crisp salad.

MAKE

Open the canned fish and drain the liquid into the sink. In the order listed, add all ingredients except the oil to a mixing bowl. Mash the ingredients together with a pastry cutter or a large fork. You may need to add more chickpea flour to get the right heft to form the mixture into patties (chickpea flour works well to bind the mixture together and also adds a crispy texture).

Divide the mixture into 8 portions and shape them into rustic patties.

Add 1 Tbsp of the oil to a skillet on medium heat. Swirl the oil around; there should be just enough to cover the bottom of the pan. Place 4 fish cakes in the pan, allowing enough space between the patties. Cook until they have browned on one side, about 3–4 minutes. Flip and brown on the other side, about 2 minutes. Remove the fish cakes to a plate and repeat with the remaining 4 patties.

Freezer-friendly instructions: Double batch this recipe and freeze what you won't eat today. Cook for half the time on either side, cool completely and freeze for up to 3 months. Thaw overnight and pan-fry on both sides for the remaining time.

HOW TO EAT
Serve with a mix of greens and pickled veggies, or as burgers in between buns of your choice.

COOKING HACK
Downsize the pan if there isn't enough oil for the patties to cook evenly.

#GOGREEN TIP
Look for canned or flash-frozen fish that has been locally or sustainably caught, or both. Find more information on page 50.

Sweets

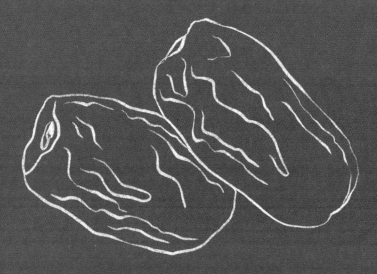

Date Kheer

V / PF
40 minutes + time to chill
Makes 8–10 servings

GATHER

20 dried dates

7 cups whole (or 2%) milk

4 green cardamom pods, crushed, green husks discarded (or ½ tsp cardamom powder)

2 Tbsp white rice, long- or short-grain, rinsed and drained

½ tsp Kashmiri (or Spanish or Iranian) saffron

1 tsp ghee

8 cashew nuts

Equipment
Immersion blender

Date *kheer* is a decadent, pudding-like, sweet dish made with dried dates and milk. There are variations of it throughout the South Asian subcontinent, but in general it's dates and rice slow-cooked with milk that makes for a luscious, decadent texture. There's one other reason to love this dish; other than the milk, all of the ingredients are accessible, affordable, and pantry stable. Plus the kheer is naturally sweetened with dates making it perfect for satisfying those after-dinner, late-night craving for sweets.

MAKE

Soak the dates in 1 cup of hot milk for 20 minutes. Seed and chop them and set them aside.

While you're waiting for the dates to plump up, pour the remaining 6 cups of milk into a heavy-bottomed saucepan and bring it to a boil on medium-high heat. Turn the heat down to medium once you see rapid bubbles form on the surface of the milk. Add the crushed cardamom and rice and cook on a slow simmer, stirring every 5 minutes or so to prevent the rice from sticking to the bottom of the pan, until the liquid is reduced to two-thirds, about 25 minutes.

Add the saffron and chopped dates to the milk mixture and cook for another 10 minutes. This allows enough time for the saffron to bloom as well as the dates to soften. Use an immersion blender to blend the kheer into a creamy texture.

While the kheer is cooking, in a separate small pan, heat the ghee on high. Once hot, turn it down to medium, add the cashew nuts, and roast them for 1 minute. Cool and chop them coarsely.

Serve the kheer in small bowls or cups, either warm or chilled (I prefer chilled), garnished with the chopped cashew nuts.

Baked Apples with Caramel Sauce

V / PF / LW
40 minutes
Makes 6 servings

GATHER

½ cup rolled oats

¼ cup sunflower seeds

¼ cup walnut pieces

1 Tbsp ghee

¼ cup brown sugar

½ tsp cinnamon powder

6 small-ish Royal Gala apples, or
   another firm, semi-sweet variety

2 cups water (approx.)

For the Caramel

½ cup organic cane sugar

1 Tbsp butter

⅓ cup heavy cream

Equipment

Mixing bowl; spice grinder; medium-
sized baking pan or dish

I adore baked apples, partly because they make an easy sweet treat, but mostly because they offer the comfort of an apple pie with none of the hard work. This recipe also uses sunflower seeds, the underhyped, constantly overlooked food that not only is fantastic for our health but also represents the root-to-seed, climate-smart spirit that we need right now. Having said that, I will let you in on a secret: it's the caramel that is the star of the show in this dish. With its sweet, buttery flavour and deep amber colour, it complements a ton of different flavours, and is perfect just the way it is.

MAKE

Preheat the oven to 375°F.

In the spice grinder, lightly crush the oats, sunflower seeds, and walnuts together into a coarse, crumbly mixture. Put the mixture in a mixing bowl and stir in the ghee, brown sugar, and cinnamon. Set aside.

Slice off the tops of the apples and set them aside. Core the apples, taking care not to cut through the bottom of the apple. Spoon the oat mixture into the apples and pack it down to fill in as much as possible. Put the apple tops back on, like little hats.

Pour the water into a medium-sized baking pan so that the level of liquid is 1 inch high. Place the stuffed apples in the water and bake for about 30 minutes. The weight and density of the apples will affect the quantity of filling needed in the fruit as well as the cooking time, so use your judgment—the apples are ready when a gentle foam starts to bubble out and the fruit starts to soften and sink into itself. Use tongs to lift the tops off and bake for the last minute of two if you like your apples a little crispy.

For the Caramel

Add the sugar to a small saucepan on medium heat. Stir slowly and frequently and allow the sugar to melt, about 3 minutes. The colour of the sugar will slowly darken and the aroma will deepen. Stay by the stove because high heat will burn the sugar. Once the sugar has melted, add the butter, watching out for the sizzle. Turn the heat off, add the cream, and allow the mixture to foam. Stir quickly and turn the heat back on to low. Whisk away any lumps that may show up. If you like your caramel pourable, turn the heat off now; if you would like the mixture to thicken, cook for another minute. Caramel, once cool, will thicken naturally.

Drizzle the caramel on top of the baked apples and enjoy. Ice cream and plain cream also pair beautifully with this dessert.

RECIPE NOTE
Leftover oat mixture? Bake it in a ramekin in the same baking pan along with the apples. Serve it with some cream on the side.

COOKING HACK
Triple batch the caramel. You will be eating it all week long.

Slow-Cooked Sweet Lentils (Daal ka Halwa)

V / PF / FF
Overnight soaking + 1 hour
Makes 8 servings

GATHER

1 cup dried yellow split lentils (moong daal)

3–4 green cardamom pods (or ½ tsp cardamom powder)

4 cups whole milk

Big pinch of Kashmiri (or Spanish or Iranian) saffron

½ cup ghee

¼ cup pistachios, shelled (optional)

¼ cup raisins (optional)

1½ cups sugar

¼ cup cashew nuts (optional)

Equipment
Mortar and pestle; heavy-duty blender, heavy-bottomed pot and a tough spatula

Daal ka halwa is a traditional South Asian dessert made from lentils, sugar, milk, and ghee and often infused with saffron and other aromatic spices. This fudgy, nutritionally dense, rich dessert takes a while to cook and so is served only on special occasions, usually in the winter. In my version, the lentils are first soaked overnight, ground into a fine paste, and then slow-cooked with milk and ghee until the mixture caramelizes and turns golden brown. I hope you enjoy it.

MAKE

Wash the lentils a couple of times. Cover them with water and soak them overnight, 6 hours minimum. During this time the lentil grains will soften and double in size.

Crush the cardamom pods with a mortar and pestle, fish out the cardamom husks, and set it all aside.

Once the lentils are done soaking, discard the water and rinse them again. Purée the soaked lentils (without water) in a blender to a fine paste. Rub the lentil mixture between your fingers; it is done when it feels like a smooth paste.

Heat a saucepan on medium-low. Add the milk, reserved cardamom husks, and saffron. Simmer for a minute or two and then turn the heat off.

In a large heavy-bottomed pot, heat the ghee on medium, add the lentil paste, and start sautéing. This step takes a while and it is important to get the lentils to the right texture, so play some music and pour yourself a glass of wine. This is also a good time to multi-task if you're prepping other things in the kitchen. The lentil paste will absorb the ghee and slowly become a thick ball of dough. Keep working away at it and use the spatula to toss the lentil "dough" every 2 minutes or so. Add ¼ cup of the saffron-infused milk every 5 minutes. Avoid transferring the cardamom husks to the the lentil mixture. This technique to cook the lentils with the scented milk is similar to making risotto. Add a little bit of the liquid at a time and go slow with much tossing. After 20 minutes the lentil paste will start to change colour from pale yellow to light brown. Continue to stir and add milk.

COOKING HACK

This technique to make halwa can also be used to make a similar sweet dish out of grated hardy vegetables. Spent carrots and green or butternut squash are good vegetables to use for this.

Cook for another 20 minutes, then add the crushed cardamom powder, shelled pistachios, and raisins (if using), and finally, the sugar. Stir and fold. Once the sugar is added, the mixture will start to come together and you'll see the difference in the texture; it will soften and smooth out. Stir and fold the halwa for another 5 minutes. The entire process of transforming the lentil paste into daal ka halwa takes approximately 45 minutes.

Roast the cashew nuts (if using) in a dry, hot pan for 5 minutes. Serve the lentil halwa warm with the nuts on top.

The halwa can be refrigerated for up to 1 week or frozen for up to 6 months.

2-Ingredient Yogurt "Mousse"

V / PF
25 minutes + overnight chilling
Makes 6 servings

GATHER

2½ cups plain yogurt
10 oz (300 mL) can sweetened
   condensed milk
½ tsp vanilla essence

Equipment
Baking tray; 6 ramekins (or similarly
sized, oven-friendly containers);
hand whisk

This hassle-free sweet is made with just two main ingredients—yogurt and condensed milk. With no eggs and no gelatin either, this custard-like dessert is quite easy to make; there's usually yogurt in my fridge and canned condensed milk in the pantry. Two ingredients, some whisking, then bake and chill. Add chocolate, vanilla, or cinnamon to bump up the flavours, or top it with fresh fruit, like sliced peaches or mango. The last is always a crowd pleaser.

MAKE

Preheat the oven to 350°F. Ready a baking tray with 2 inches of warm water covering the bottom of the tray. Place 6 ramekins in the water and set aside.

Whisk together the yogurt and condensed milk to dissolve any lumps and allow air to fold gently into the mixture. Start slow with the whisk to blend and then move faster, 30–40 times. Avoid using a blender or mixer.

Add the vanilla essence and whisk a few more times until well combined.

Pour the mixture into the ramekins. Put the tray in the oven and bake until the top of the pudding turns a very pale golden colour, 15–18 minutes. Insert a thin, small knife to check if it's cooked through. Take the baking pan out of the oven and allow it to cool for 10 minutes.

Chill the ramekins in the fridge overnight.

HOW TO EAT
Serve chilled with fresh fruit slices or a sprinkle of cinnamon sugar. My kids love it plain, just as it is.

Shahi Tukda Made with Leftover Bread

V / LW
45 minutes + chilling time
Makes 6 servings

GATHER

7 cups whole (or 2%) milk

4 green cardamom pods, coarsely crushed, green husks discarded (or ½ tsp cardamom powder)

⅔ cup sugar

½ tsp Kashmiri (or Spanish or Iranian) saffron

3 Tbsp + 1 tsp ghee

¼ cup sliced pistachios

6 slices white (or whole wheat) bread

2 whole green cardamom pods

Rose petals to taste

#GOGREEN TIP
Use leftover gluten-free or whole grain bread and make this sumptuous dessert work for your family's needs.

Literally translated as "royal serving," *shahi tukda* is worth making just for the spiced milk *rabri* alone. The milk is gently simmered, infused with saffron, then sweetened and cooked for half an hour to reduce the liquid to an almost custardy mixture that can be enjoyed on its own or used in any number of ways. Rabri adds a bright sparkle to this recipe, in which bread slices toasted in ghee are covered with the spiced milk rabri mixture. Garnished with rose petals and chopped nuts, this is an exceptional dessert fit for royalty despite often being made with leftover pieces of bread.

MAKE

Pour the milk into a heavy-bottomed saucepan on medium-high and bring to a boil. Turn the heat down to medium-low once you see rapid bubbles form. Add the crushed cardamom and cook the milk low and slow, stirring every 5 minutes and scraping the bottom to prevent it from sticking and burning. Reduce the quantity of the mixture by half, about 30 minutes. Add the sugar and saffron and allow the mixture to infuse and simmer for another 5 minutes. Then turn the heat off and set aside.

While the rabri is cooking, in a separate skillet, heat 1 tsp of the ghee on medium, turn the heat to low, and roast the pistachios until gently browned, about 1 minute. Set aside.

Prepare the bread by slicing away the crusts (use the sides for the recipes on page 146) and cutting it into triangles.

In a large skillet, heat 1 Tbsp of the ghee on medium and add the green cardamom pods to flavour the fat. Discard. Fry the bread in batches until the slices are pale brown. Add ghee as needed and avoid overcrowding the pan.

Arrange the toast in a shallow dish. Pour the warm rabri over them, allowing enough liquid to soak through the bread. Garnish with roasted pistachios and rose petals.

Refrigerate and serve chilled.

Glossary

atta
Wholemeal wheat flour widely used for roti or chapatti.

besan (also known as **gram flour**)
Chickpea flour made from roasted and ground split chickpeas. It makes a great swap for all-purpose flour in many dishes and adds a robust, almost nutty flavour. Chickpea flour is much higher in protein, fibre and other nutritional benefits than other commonly used flours.

chapatti (also known as **roti** or **phulka**)
An unleavened flat yet puffy bread that is a staple food in many parts of South Asia. It is made from a simple dough of whole wheat flour and water that is kneaded, allowed to rest, and then rolled into thin circles and cooked on a hot skillet or *tawa*. Chapattis are typically eaten with a variety of curries, vegetables, and lentils and are often used instead of a spoon to scoop the food. See the recipe on page 99.

daal (also spelled **dal** or **dhal**)
A Hindi/Urdu word widely used in South Asian cuisine to refer to a stewy, soupy dish made with dried pulses, such as lentils, peas, or beans. This dish that is mostly made with simple ingredients and few steps is a rich source of protein and fibre. It is a staple food in many cultures around South Asia, the Caribbean Islands, and parts of Africa. Daal is often served with chapatti or rice. See the recipe on page 181.

dahi
The Hindi word for plain yogurt. See the recipe on pages 84–85.

ghee
A cooking fat commonly used in South Asian cuisine. It can be made using two different techniques. In North America, it is often referred to as clarified butter and is made by simmering butter until the milk solids separate. Another, more traditional way, and how my mom makes it, is with cream instead of butter. This cream, collected over multiple days from boiled and then refrigerated (whole) milk, is simmered until the milk solids separate. In both techniques, a golden-coloured liquid is left behind. This liquid has a deep, nutty flavour and a high smoke point and turns into a cloudy solid at room temperature. Per traditional wisdom, ghee is considered to be a healthier alternative to many other cooking fats.

kadhai (also spelled **kadai** or **kadhahi**)
A type of deep, circular cooking pan commonly used in South Asian cuisine. It is typically made of cast iron or stainless steel, though aluminum is also quite common. The shape and depth of the kadhai make it suitable for dishes that take a lot of tossing and stirring, and for sautéing, preparing curries, and deep-frying. It is similar to the wok used in East Asian cuisines but deeper with higher sides and two small handles instead of one long one.

kebab
These come in all different shapes, but mostly they are round or oval-shaped grilled patties made with minced meat, mashed lentils, vegetables, and spices.

paneer

Unripened, non-melting, fresh cheese made from milk. Paneer is made by heating the milk, adding some acid (I use lime juice), and then simmering it until the milk solids separate from the whey. Paneer is widely available in India as a healthy and vegetarian alternative to meat protein. It is eaten in many ways, fresh or cooked using whole spices, onions, and tomatoes. See the recipe to make paneer on page 95.

paraat (also spelled **parat**)

A large, flat, circular tray or plate with high sides. It is traditionally made of brass or stainless steel and is used for kneading dough to prepare chapattis or rotis (flat, circular breads). The wide, flat surface of the paraat allows space for easy kneading of the dough, and its high sides prevent the dough from spilling over.

peda

A Hindi word for a small disc shape. Mostly, the word is used to describe a piece of dough used to make chapatti, Indian flatbread. It is also a type of traditional Indian sweet made from *khoa* (a type of milk solid), sugar, saffron, cardamom, and nuts. In this book, it is in relation to the first reference.

raita

A side dish, almost like a dip, that is often made with plain yogurt, chopped cucumber, mint, salt, and cumin powder.

steam tunnels

Holes that form while cooking whole grains and lentils. One common method to cook grains like rice, quinoa, millet, and barley is boiling them in water, then reducing the heat and covering the saucepan with a lid to trap steam. With the right proportion of liquid to grain, the water will be absorbed and vertical holes will form through the grain. These are steam tunnels and when you see them you know the grains are almost done, and are likely tender and fluffy. Turn the heat off, leave the lid on, and set the pan aside for five minutes before eating.

tadka

A cooking technique of frying spices in hot oil or ghee, sometimes along with garlic, onion, curry leaves, or diced tomatoes. The hot mixture is added to main dishes at sizzling temperatures to enhance the dishes' flavour and aroma. Traditionally tadka is used for lentils and cooked vegetables, but I often use it in salads and on chutneys to enhance the flavour and texture.

tawa (also spelled **tava**)

A flat, circular skillet or frying pan, typically made of cast iron or non-stick materials, used for cooking chapatti, roti, pancakes, or dosa. The tawa has a flat cooking surface that allows for high, even heat and can be placed directly on a stovetop or over an open flame.

Notes

PREFACE

1. Gayle Spinazze, "Press Release: Doomsday Clock Set at 90 Seconds to Midnight," *Bulletin of the Atomic Scientists*, January 24, 2023, https://thebulletin.org/2023/01/press-release-doomsday-clock-set-at-90-seconds-to-midnight/.

AN INTRODUCTION, A STORY OF ROOT SHOCK, AND A LOVE LETTER OF SORTS

1. Food and Mood: Improving Mental Health through Diet and Nutrition, online course, Food and Mood Centre, Deakin University, https://foodandmoodcentre.com.au/academy/online-courses/.

WHAT TO EXPECT IN THIS BOOK

1. "The Planetary Health Diet," EAT, https://eatforum.org/learn-and-discover/the-planetary-health-diet/
2. Felice Jacka, *Brain Changer: How Diet Can Save Your Mental Health* (London: Yellow Kite, 2019). Dr. Jacka is the director of the Food and Mood Centre at Deakin University in Australia and the founder and president of the International Society for Nutritional Psychiatry Research.
3. Sustainable Development Goals, United Nations Department of Economic and Social Affairs, https://sdgs.un.org/goals.

CHAPTER 1: THE BIG WHY

1. Ashkan Afshin et al., "Health Effects of Dietary Risks in 195 Countries, 1990–2017: A Systematic Analysis for the Global Burden of Disease Study 2017," *Lancet* 393, no. 10184 (May 11, 2019): 1958–72, https://doi.org/10.1016/S0140-6736(19)30041-8.
2. Natasha Bray, "The Microbiota–Gut–Brain Axis," *Nature Portfolio*, June 17, 2019, https://www.nature.com/articles/d42859-019-00021-3.
3. United Nations, *Policy Brief: COVID-19 and the Need for Action on Mental Health*, May 13, 2020, https://unsdg.un.org/sites/default/files/2020-05/UN-Policy-Brief-COVID-19-and-mental-health.pdf.

4. SMILES Trial: Felice N. Jacka et al., "A Randomised Controlled Trial of Dietary Improvement for Adults with Major Depression (the 'SMILES' Trial)," *BMC Medicine* 15, no. 23 (2017), https://doi.org/10.1186/s12916-017-0791-y.
5. IPCC, 2019: Summary for Policymakers. In: Climate Change and Land: an IPCC special report on climate change, desertification, land degradation, sustainable land management, food security, and greenhouse gas fluxes in terrestrial ecosystems [P.R. Shukla, et al (eds.)]. In press https://www.ipcc.ch/srccl/.
6. "IPCC: The Call to Action Cannot Be Ignored," EAT, https://eatforum.org/learn-and-discover/ipcc-the-call-to-action-cannot-be-ignored.
7. "The EAT-*Lancet* Commission on Food, Planet, Health," EAT, https://eatforum.org/eat-lancet-commission/.
8. "The EAT-*Lancet* Commission Summary Report," https://eatforum.org/content/uploads/2019/07/EAT-Lancet_Commission_Summary_Report.pdf.

CHAPTER 2: THE BIG HOW

1. "What is Agrobiodiversity?" (fao.org) https://www.fao.org/3/y5609e/y5609e02.htm.
2. "Save Our Food Biodiversity," Slow Food International, August 9, 2013, https://www.slowfood.com/save-our-food-biodiversity/.
3. *The Global Risks Report 2020*, World Economic Forum, https://www.weforum.org/reports/the-global-risks-report-2020.
4. Oliver Milman, "Meat Accounts for Nearly 60% of All Greenhouse Gases from Food Production, Study Finds," *Guardian*, September 13, 2021, https://www.theguardian.com/environment/2021/sep/13/meat-greenhouses-gases-food-production-study.
5. Janet Ranganathan and Richard Waite, "Sustainable Diets: What You Need to Know in 12 Charts," World Resources Institute, April 20, 2016, https://www.wri.org/insights/sustainable-diets-what-you-need-know-12-charts.
6. Mark Bittman's thoughts on how to replace meat: Mark Bittman, Charlie Mitchell, and Melissa McCart, "How to Replace Meat," Bittman Project, May 4, 2021, https://www.bittmanproject.com/p/how-to-replace-meat.

7. Lori Nikkel et al., *The Avoidable Crisis of Food Waste: The Roadmap*; Second Harvest and Value Chain Management International; Ontario, Canada, https://www.secondharvest.ca/getmedia/73121ee2-5693-40ec-b6cc-dba6ac9c6756/The-Avoidable-Crisis-of-Food-Waste-Roadmap.pdf.

8. "Tackling Food Loss and Waste: A Triple Win Opportunity," Food and Agriculture Organization of the United Nations, September 29, 2022, https://www.fao.org/newsroom/detail/FAO-UNEP-agriculture-environment-food-loss-waste-day-2022/en.

9. Energy, Food and Agriculture Organization of the United Nations (fao.org), https://www.fao.org/energy/home/en/.

10. Food Waste Food Print, FAO.org, News Article: Food wastage: Key facts and figures, https://www.fao.org/news/story/en/item/196402/icode/.

11. Plastics found in lungs: Lauren C. Jenner et al., "Detection of Microplastics in Human Lung Tissue Using µFTIR Spectroscopy," *Science of the Total Environment* 831 (2022): 154907, https://doi.org/10.1016/j.scitotenv.2022.154907.

12. Instant-noodle shortage: Aisyah Llewellyn, "Far from Ukraine, Indonesia's Favourite Noodles Run Out of Stock," *Al Jazeera*, March 21, 2022, https://www.aljazeera.com/news/2022/3/21/as-ukraine-war-sends-wheat-pas-indonesians-asking-wheres-indomie.

13. True cost accounting principles: "True Cost Accounting: The Real Cost of Cheap Food," *The Lexicon of Sustainability*, PBS Food, https://www.pbs.org/food/features/lexicon-of-sustainability-true-cost-accounting-the-real-cost-of-cheap-food/.

14. Damian Carrington, "Avoiding Meat and Dairy Is 'Single-Biggest Way' to Reduce Your Impact on Earth," *Guardian*, May 31, 2018, https://www.theguardian.com/environment/2018/may/31/avoiding-meat-and-dairy-is-single-biggest-way-to-reduce-your-impact-on-earth.

15. Hannah Ritchie, "Is Organic Really Better for the Environment Than Conventional Agriculture?," Our World in Data, October 19, 2017, https://ourworldindata.org/is-organic-agriculture-better-for-the-environment.

16. Hannah Ritchie, "Less Meat Is Nearly Always Better Than Sustainable Meat, to Reduce Your Carbon Footprint," Our World in Data, February 4, 2020, https://ourworldindata.org/less-meat-or-sustainable-meat.

17. Degradation of topsoil: "FAO Warns 90 Per Cent of Earth's Topsoil at Risk by 2050," UN News, United Nations, July 27, 2022, https://news.un.org/en/story/2022/07/1123462.

18. Tulane University study: Keith Brannon, "Swapping Just One Item Can Make Diets Substantially More Planet-Friendly," *Tulane News*, January 13, 2022, https://news.tulane.edu/pr/swapping-just-one-item-can-make-diets-substantially-more-planet-friendly.

19. Joe Fassler, "Inside Big Beef's Climate Messaging Machine: Confuse, Defend and Downplay," *Guardian*, May 3, 2023 https://www.theguardian.com/environment/2023/may/03/beef-industry-public-relations-messaging-machine.

CHAPTER 3: HOW TO STOCK A GOOD FOOD KITCHEN

1. California almond industry: Associated Press, "Climate Change in California Is Threatening the World's Top Almond Producer," NPR, August 17, 2021, https://www.npr.org/2021/08/17/1028452988climate-change-california-drought-heat-almond-production.

2. "Americans Are Eating More Ultra-processed Foods," New York University, October 14, 2021, https://www.nyu.edu/about/news-publications/news/2021/october/ultra-processed-foods.html.

CHAPTER 4: RECIPES WITH ALL THE BENEFITS

1. "Chia Seeds," Nutrition Source, Harvard T. H. Chan School of Public Health, https://www.hsph.harvard.edu/nutritionsource/food-features/chia-seeds/.

2. "Lettuce," Agricultural Marketing Resource Center, revised November 2021, https://www.agmrc.org/commodities-products/vegetables/lettuce.

Recommended Reading

- Anatomy of Action, a movement to help people contribute to Sustainable Development Goal 12, responsible consumption and production, https://www.anatomyofaction.org/.

- Beans Is How, a movement to motivate people around the world to recognize the value of beans in a sustainable, healthy diets, https://sdg2 advocacyhub.org/news/beans-how.

- David Suzuki Foundation, a non-profit, evidence-based research and education organization, https://davidsuzuki.org/.

- Heather M. Francis et al., "A Brief Diet Intervention Can Reduce Symptoms of Depression in Young Adults—a Randomised Controlled Trial," *PLoS ONE* 14, no. 10 (2019): e0222768, https://doi.org/10.1371/journal .pone.0222768.

- Intergovernmental Panel on Climate Change, Climate Change and Land: An IPCC Special Report on Climate Change, Desertification, Land Degradation, Sustainable Land Management, Food Security, and Greenhouse Gas Fluxes in Terrestrial Ecosystems, 2019, https://www.ipcc .ch/srccl/.

- SeafoodWatch, a global organization that offers science-based seafood recommendations for consumers and the food industry, https://www .seafoodwatch.org/.

- How do I make sense of food date labels? Love Food Hate Waste, Best Before Labels | Love Food Hate Waste, https://lovefoodhatewaste.ca/about /resources/.

- One or all of these books by Vandana Shiva, Indian scientist and environmental activist who founded the Research Foundation for Science, Technology, and Natural Resource Policy, an organization devoted to developing sustainable methods of agriculture. Subsequently, she launched Navdanya, a series of seed banks in India to combat the growing trend of monoculture, https://www.navdanya.org/.
  - *Who Really Feeds the World*, 2016
  - *Oneness vs. The 1%*, 2018
  - *Making Peace With the Earth*, 2012

- Sustainable Food Trust, *The Hidden Cost of UK Food*, revised edition, 2019, https://sustainable foodtrust.org/wp-content/uploads/2022/01 /Website-Version-The-Hidden-Cost-of-UK-Food _compressed.pdf.

- World Wildlife Fund and Knorr, *Future 50 Foods: 50 Foods for Healthier People and a Healthier Planet*, February 2019, https://www.wwf.org.uk /sites/default/files/2019-02/Knorr_Future_50 _Report_FINAL_Online.pdf.

- Become a Reducetarian, https://www.reducetarian .org/.

Acknowledgements

This book has been a dream in the making for years. Good food for all is, has been, and must continue to be a community effort that requires the power of the collective. I'm grateful to have had friends, family, and colleagues hold my hand at various stages in the process—more people than I can remember, I'm sure, but I will try regardless.

To the talented and patient team at TouchWood Editions. To Tori Elliott for your unfailing generosity and expertise. Thank you for your openness, big-picture focus, and steady guidance through this journey. To Taryn Boyd, our work together was brief but I am grateful that you agreed to take the chance on a newbie writer and her ambitious dream. Kate Kennedy for keeping it all straight. I think—no, I'm sure—without you, things (and I!) would have fallen apart. Meg Yamamoto for your speedy and careful work. Your thoughtful eye gave the book a polish that I didn't know was missing. Thank you for asking me, "Do you mean to say . . ." again and again. Thank you also for starting the first round of edits with encouraging words that helped me remember why I was doing this at all. Senica Maltese for pulling it all together. And for helping me articulate a sentence that I had been struggling with for months. Curtis Samuel, for your enthusiasm and marketing skills, helping this book reach far and wide. To Jazmin Welch, for your incredible illustrations that connected the content in a way that I had not imagined possible. Thank you also for your cover design and for bringing the spirit of the book to the forefront. No small task.

To Diana Muresan, the book's photographer, whose creative expertise and remarkable talent for connecting people with food and bringing out the best in both helped me tell a deeply authentic story. I'm so grateful for our work together!

To Radhika V. Bhogaraju for helping me stay accountable. Thank you for your sharp eye for detail on an early stage of the book.

To my agent, James McGowan, who I met on a gloomy November day on Zoom and who saw in my book proposal a dream worth championing. I cannot overstate my gratitude and how lucky I feel to have you in my corner.

To Sara Smeaton, with her boundless generosity and love and so much more. Thank you for untangling the yarn for me more times than I can remember.

To Priyanka Singh, with her big heart and so much more. Thank you for the joy and ease with which you try what I cook. And for having the best ideas for dining out when I'm tired of cooking.

Thank you to all the scientists and researchers, some of whom I have credited in the book, for sharing your expertise with the world and for helping connect the dots for the rest of us.

To all the farmers, growers, gardeners, and nature workers. Thank you for the vision, fortitude, and courage it takes to imagine the possibilities that lie under the soil when most just see the dirt.

For the people in the Maple and Marigold community for your years of affection. For helping to test and taste dishes. I am a better recipe writer and storyteller because of your feedback.

To my family. Vivek, Mahika, and Saranya. For trying all the new dishes especially the unsuccessful ones, like the "none of the meat" scotch eggs. For your patience and cheerful support during the long months of "the kitchen is not available right now." For your willingness to juggle wi-fi and the nimble ducking out of the frame just as "Hi, it's Puneeta, I'm here in my kitchen" livestreams began. And for so much more. This book is dedicated to you.

Conversion Chart

VOLUME

IMPERIAL	METRIC
⅛ tsp	0.5 mL
¼ tsp	1 mL
½ tsp	2.5 mL
¾ tsp	4 mL
1 tsp	5 mL
½ Tbsp	8 mL
1 Tbsp	15 mL
1½ Tbsp	23 mL
2 Tbsp	30 mL
2½ Tbsp	38 mL
¼ cup	60 mL
⅓ cup	80 mL
½ cup	125 mL
⅔ cup	165 mL
¾ cup	185 mL
1 cup	250 mL
1¼ cups	310 mL
1⅓ cups	330 mL
1½ cups	375 mL
1⅔ cups	415 mL
1¾ cups	435 mL
2 cups / 1 pint	500 mL
2¼ cups	560 mL
2⅓ cups	580 mL
2½ cups	625 mL
2⅔ cups	665 mL
2¾ cups	690 mL
3 cups	750 mL
3½ cups	875 mL
4 cups	1 L
5 cups	1.25 L
6 cups	1.5 L
8 cups / 2 quarts	2 L
25 cups	6 L

WEIGHT

IMPERIAL	METRIC
1 oz	30 g
4 oz	115 g
8 oz	225 g
10 oz	250 g
12 oz	340 g
1 lb (16 oz)	450 g
2 lb	900 g
5 lb	2,250 g

CANS

IMPERIAL	METRIC
6 oz	177mL
10 oz	284 mL
11oz	300ml
14 oz	398 mL
16 oz	480 mL
28 oz	796 mL

OVEN TEMPERATURE

IMPERIAL	METRIC
200°F	95°C
225°F	105°C
250°F	120°C
275°F	135°C
300°F	150°C
325°F	160°C
350°F	180°C
375°F	190°C
400°F	200°C
425°F	220°C
450°F	230°C

LENGTH/WIDTH

IMPERIAL	METRIC
1/12 inch	2 mm
⅛ inch	3 mm
⅙ inch	4 mm
¼ inch	6 mm
½ inch	12 mm
¾ inch	2 cm
1 inch	2.5 cm
1½ inches	3.5 cm
2 inches	5 cm
2½ inches	6.5 cm
3 inches	7.5 cm
3½ inches	9 cm
4 inches	10 cm
5 inches	12.5 cm
6 inches	15 cm
7 inches	18 cm
8 inches	20 cm
9 inches	23 cm
10 inches	25 cm

TEMPERATURE

(For oven temperatures, see chart below)

IMPERIAL	METRIC
115°F	46°C
150°F	66°C
160°F	71°C
170°F	77°C
180°F	82°C
185°F	85°C
190°F	88°C
200°F	93°C
240°F	116°C
247°F	119°C
250°F	121°C
290°F	143°C
300°F	149°C
350°F	177°C
360°F	182°C
370°F	188°C

US FLUID OUNCES

US FLUID OUNCES	US CUSTOMARY	METRIC
¼ oz	½ Tbsp / 1½ tsp	7.5 mL
⅓ oz	2 tsp	10 mL
½ oz	1 Tbsp	15 mL
¾ oz	1½ Tbsp / 4½ tsp	22 mL
1 oz (1 shot)	2 Tbsp	30 mL
1¼ oz	2½ Tbsp	37.5 mL
1½ oz	3 Tbsp	45 mL
2 oz	¼ cup	60 mL
2½ oz	5 Tbsp	75 mL
3 oz	¼ cup + 2 Tbsp	90 mL
3½ oz	¼ cup + 3 Tbsp	105 mL
4 oz	½ cup	125 mL
4½ oz	½ cup + 1 Tbsp	140 mL
5 oz	½ cup + 2 Tbsp	155 mL

Index

K. 2024.